100 Days

Of

Pre Algebra
Practice
Workbook

Order Of Operations

How many times have you evaluated a numerical expression, and even though you know your division, multiplication, addition, and subtraction is correct, you still have the wrong answer?

If this has happened to you, then you probably haven't used the order of operations correctly.

The **order of operations** is a **set of rules** that you must follow in order to correctly evaluate a numerical expression that contains multiple operations (a combination of addition, subtraction, multiplication, and division).
To remember this set of rules we use the acronym: **PEMDAS**

So what is PEMDAS? And how it helps us to remember the rules when using the order of operations?

PEMDAS: Parentheses, Exponents, Multiplication or Division and Addition or Subtraction.

PEMDAS

P=Parenthesis

E=Exponents

M=Multiplication

D=Division

A=Addition

S=Subtraction

The order of the letters in PEMDAS tells you what to calculate first, second, third and so on, until the calculation is complete.

A phrase has been attached with the letters in PEMDAS: **P**lease **E**xcuse **M**y **D**ear **A**unt **S**ally

If you can remember this phrase, then it may be easier to remember the order of operations given in PEMDAS

PEMDAS

The order of operations

- Always perform parenthesis and/or groups first
- After parenthesis and groupings, perform exponents
- After parenthesis and exponents, perform multiplication/division (**whichever comes first moving from left to right**)
- After multiplication/division, perform addition and/or subtraction (**whichever comes first moving from left to right**)

Let's look at a few examples of how to correctly use PEMDAS to perform the order of operations.

Example 1: (2 + 3) x 4

Solve what is inside the parentheses first. In this case, 2+3=5.

Then perform multiplication: 5 x 4 = 20

$$(2 + 3) \text{ x } 4$$
$$5 \text{ x } 4 = 20$$

Example 2: 16 ÷ (9 - 7)^2

Solve what is inside the parentheses first. In this case, 9 - 7= 2.

Then move onto the exponents: 2 ^2 = 4

Finally perform division 16 ÷ 4 = 4

$$16 ÷ (9 - 7)\text{^}2$$
$$16 ÷ 2\text{^}2$$
$$16 ÷ 4 \quad = 4$$

Example 3:   8 x 4 + 3

According to PEMDAS, you have to perform multiplication/division before addition/subtraction, so: 8 x 4 = 32

Then perform addition: 32 + 3 = 35

8 x 4 + 3

32 + 3 = 35

Example 4:   50 - 5 x 2

According to PEMDAS, you have to perform multiplication/division before addition/subtraction, so in this case you do not perform operations from left to right.but you need to perform multiplication first: 5 x 2 = 10

Then move onto subtraction: 50 - 10 = 40

50 - 5 x 2

50 - 10 = 40

Example 5:   3 x 4 ÷ 2

Remember that PEMDAS requires you to solve Multiplication/Division from left to right based on whichever comes first.In this example multiplication comes first so you would first perform: 3 x 4 = 12

Then perform division: 12÷ 2 = 6

$$3 \times 4 \div 2$$
$$12 \div 2 = 6$$

Example 6:   50 ÷ 5 x 2

According to PEMDAS, you need to perform multiplication/division from left to right based on whichever comes first, so in this case division comes first, so: 50 ÷ 5 = 10

Then move onto multiplication: 10 x 2 = 20

$$50 \div 5 \times 2$$
$$10 \times 2 = 20$$

Many students fail to use PEMDAS correctly in these kinds of examples and perform multiplication first

50÷5x2 = 50÷10 = 5 = **wrong answer**

I hope this helps in your study of order of operations.

Please leave a review because we would love to hear your feedback, opinions, and advice to create better products and services for you!

You are greatly appreciated!

1) 12 + 16 - 9 + 17

2) 3 - 1 x 4 + 2

3) 11 + 11 x 3 + 5

4) 5 x 9 + 5 + 14

5) 14 + 19 x 6 + 19

6) 14 x 9 + 5 + 18

7) 9 + 2 x 3 + 17

8) 4 + 18 x 2 + 6

9) 7 + 18 x 8 - 2

10) 3 x 17 + 9 + 13

1) 2 + 18 - 10 x 9

2) 18 - 15 x 11 + 13

3) 9 x 6 - 6 + 7

4) 2 + 6 - 1 + 9

5) 18 x 19 + 3 + 15

6) 5 + 7 x 17 - 10

7) 5 + 8 x 10 + 15

8) 9 x 4 - 2 + 17

9) 4 + 10 x 17 - 5

10) 8 x 18 + 16 + 8

Day 3	**Name:**_____	**Score:**_____

1) 18 - 13 + 6 + 13

2) 16 + 6 + 11 - 2

3) 6 + 12 - 12 x 7

4) 12 + 9 + 6 - 5

5) 3 + 11 x 10 + 10

6) 16 - 15 + 12 + 2

7) 18 + 14 - 6 + 10

8) 2 + 8 + 19 - 13

9) 8 + 6 - 3 x 19

10) 17 x 12 + 16 - 5

1) 19 x 19 + 15 + 2

6) 14 + 4 x 9 - 9

2) 9 - 3 x 13 + 12

7) 14 - 3 + 12 x 10

3) 13 x 18 + 4 + 7

8) 12 + 5 + 8 x 12

4) 17 - 12 + 5 + 13

9) 16 x 15 - 4 + 3

5) 17 + 12 + 16 - 10

10) 14 + 4 + 11 x 5

1) 9 + 8 x 2 +12

6) 2 - 1 +11 + 9

2) 13 + 6 x 10 +12

7) 14 x 19 + 6 +17

3) 4 x 4 - 1 +16

8) 2 +13 - 2 x 8

4) 2 - 1 + 8 + 6

9) 15 +19 + 5 - 1

5) 4 x 3 +15 +11

10) 5 + 4 - 3 + 3

Day 6

Name:_____

Score:
_____

1) 16 - 14 + 13 x 7

2) 2 - 1 + 19 + 18

3) 9 x 8 + 4 + 19

4) 13 x 17 + 19 - 18

5) 5 + 12 x 18 + 13

6) 12 + 11 - 8 + 11

7) 16 + 7 + 7 - 3

8) 8 - 5 x 6 + 17

9) 14 - 3 + 12 + 2

10) 17 + 19 + 17 x 11

Day 7	**Name:**_____	Score: _____

1) 10 + 12 x 17 + 17

2) 19 + 18 + 2 - 1

3) 18 - 11 x 17 + 2

4) 4 x 11 + 2 + 5

5) 15 + 17 - 12 x 6

6) 2 + 11 - 5 + 10

7) 15 x 16 + 16 + 12

8) 8 + 16 + 18 x 16

9) 12 - 6 + 16 + 3

10) 3 - 2 x 16 + 17

1) $11 - 8 \times 10 + 12$

2) $5 - 1 + 12 + 16$

3) $5 - 3 + 15 \times 5$

4) $8 \times 9 + 3 - 3$

5) $18 + 3 + 2 - 1$

6) $16 \times 8 + 7 + 17$

7) $14 + 15 \times 7 - 5$

8) $13 + 7 + 5 \times 9$

9) $7 + 18 - 5 \times 19$

10) $19 \times 13 - 7 + 6$

	Score:
Day 9	**Name:** _____

1) 15 + 2 - 1 x 11

2) 15 - 13 + 8 x 5

3) 11 + 18 - 5 x 18

4) 2 + 17 x 16 + 14

5) 3 + 18 + 19 - 19

6) 18 x 8 - 3 + 12

7) 10 - 3 x 8 + 13

8) 8 x 12 + 6 - 2

9) 6 x 17 - 13 + 13

10) 4 - 2 x 18 + 3

Name:_____

Score:
_____

1) 13 x 12 - 1 + 14

6) 8 + 17 + 11 - 6

2) 14 - 6 x 3 + 15

7) 9 + 15 + 3 x 10

3) 19 - 12 + 18 + 11

8) 2 + 18 x 13 - 8

4) 7 - 6 x 9 + 10

9) 15 x 5 + 7 - 3

5) 6 - 5 + 9 x 7

10) 15 + 11 x 18 - 16

1) (17 + 4) x 8 + 6

2) 10 x 8 +(7 - 7)

3) (9 + 5)+ 15 x 3

4) (12 +25 - 5) x 16

5) (14 + 6) x (7 + 5)

6) (11 + 3) x 10 + 4

7) 4 x 5 +(6 + 5)

8) (16 + 3)+ 16 x 2

9) (12 +23 - 3) x 16

10) (12 + 7) x (13 + 2)

Day 12	Name:	Score:

1) (15 - 8) x 14 + 2

2)   6 x 4 +(8 - 5)

3) (12 - 5)+ 10 x 2

4) (13 +33 - 6) x 8

5) (11 + 2) x(7 - 3)

6) (14 + 5) x 8 - 5

7)   7 x 11 +(6 + 7)

8) (16 - 3)+ 14 x 7

9) (14 +48 - 2) x 3

10) (11 + 3) x(8 - 2)

Name:_____

Score:
_____

1) $(16 - 7) \times 9 + 4$

2) $7 \times 4 + (8 - 8)$

3) $(9 + 5) + 20 \times 2$

4) $(13 + 41 - 4) \times 10$

5) $(8 + 4) \times (10 - 3)$

6) $(19 + 4) \times 8 - 3$

7) $2 \times 8 + (10 - 6)$

8) $(11 + 5) + 24 \times 4$

9) $(12 + 22 - 2) \times 2$

10) $(13 + 6) \times (9 - 5)$

Day 14	Name:	Score:

1) (19 - 2) x 9 + 3

6) (15 + 6) x 13 - 2

2) 10 x 4 +(5 + 5)

7) 9 x 12 +(3 +10)

3) (12 - 3)+ 20 x 4

8) (11 + 5)+ 8 x 2

4) (8 +28 - 6) x 10

9) (11 +34 - 5) x 4

5) (9 + 2) x(10 - 4)

10) (14 + 6) x(8 + 4)

Day 15	Name:	Score:

1) (14 - 7) x 10 - 4

2)   6 x 10 +(2 + 7)

3) (12 + 4) + 16 x 4

4) (8 +33 - 5) x 12

5) (13 + 3) x (14 - 2)

6) (19 - 4) x 14 - 4

7)   10 x 12 +(9 - 10)

8) (11 + 3) + 12 x 2

9) (15 +39 - 4) x 2

10) (8 + 3) x (13 - 5)

1) (13 - 3) x 12 - 5

2) 6 x 13 +(8 - 4)

3) (16 + 4)+ 14 x 2

4) (12 + 17 - 5) x 12

5) (11 + 6) x (7 - 5)

6) (20 - 7) x 9 + 4

7) 9 x 13 +(7 + 9)

8) (16 - 5)+ 10 x 2

9) (13 + 17 - 6) x 3

10) (12 + 6) x (11 + 2)

1) (18 + 7) x 13 - 5

6) (20 - 5) x 12 + 2

2)   6 x 6 +(5 - 2)

7)   5 x 3 +(7 + 3)

3) (16 -   2)+ 15 x 5

8) (13 -   2)+ 16 x 8

4) (8 +45 - 5) x 8

9) (8 +30 - 2) x 3

5) (11 + 6) x(13 - 3)

10) (15 + 7) x(9 + 2)

1) $(18 - 8) \times 13 - 4$

2) $7 \times 2 + (8 - 5)$

3) $(10 - 5) + 14 \times 2$

4) $(13 + 25 - 2) \times 9$

5) $(15 + 5) \times (7 - 5)$

6) $(17 + 3) \times 12 - 4$

7) $9 \times 12 + (5 - 4)$

8) $(11 - 2) + 14 \times 2$

9) $(8 + 29 - 5) \times 16$

10) $(8 + 7) \times (9 + 2)$

1) (11 + 2) x 10 + 2

2)   10 x 8 +(9 + 7)

3) (16 + 4) + 24 x 12

4) (14 + 18 - 4) x 2

5) (11 + 5) x (12 - 3)

6) (16 - 8) x 12 + 2

7)   9 x 2 +(2 - 9)

8) (13 - 4) + 8 x 2

9) (15 + 13 - 4) x 4

10) (15 + 6) x (14 + 2)

1) (15 - 6) x 10 - 4

6) (12 + 4) x 10 + 4

2)   10 x 8 +(9 - 10)

7)   4 x 7 +(3 - 4)

3) (9 + 4)+ 16 x 8

8) (11 + 2)+ 16 x 2

4) (12 +40 - 4) x 6

9) (15 +19 - 6) x 7

5) (8 + 7) x(14 - 3)

10) (11 + 7) x(9 - 2)

Day 21	**Name:** _____	**Score:** ____

1) $(8 \times 4 + 4^2) - 2$

2) $5 \times (10 - 5) + 3^2$

3) $(14 - 5)^2 + (8 - 4)$

4) $(44 - 4^2) - (16 - 2)$

5) $(30 - 2) - 2 + 7^2$

6) $(57 - 5^2) - (9 - 5)$

7) $(11 - 5)^2 + (12 - 3)$

8) $(32 - 2) - 2 - 3^2$

9) $6 \times (13 - 6) + 7^2$

10) $(9 \times 10 - 8^2) + 7$

Day 22	**Name**:_____	Score:_____

1) $6 \times (9 + 2) - 9^2$

2) $(54 - 2^2) - (3 + 7)$

3) $(55 - 5^2) - (17 - 2)$

4) $(6 \times 7 + 3^2) + 10$

5) $(34 - 6) - 2 + 4^2$

6) $(10 - 4)^2 + (8 - 2)$

7) $(30 - 2) - 14 + 7^2$

8) $(9 + 2)^2 + (12 - 3)$

9) $(7 \times 9 - 4^2) + 7$

10) $2 \times (8 + 3) - 3^2$

1) $(3 + 4)^2 + (12 - 4)$

6) $5 \times (8 + 5) + 2^2$

2) $5 \times (10 + 6) + 3^2$

7) $(13 \times 8 - 6^2) - 5$

3) $(26 - 2) - 2 + 7^2$

8) $(7 \times 5 + 8^2) - 10$

4) $(64 - 4) - 20 - 5^2$

9) $(40 - 2^2) - (12 - 6)$

5) $(76 - 6^2) - (5 + 5)$

10) $(9 + 3)^2 + (12 - 3)$

Day 24	**Name**:_____	**Score:** ___

1) $(54 - 2^2) - (27 - 2)$

2) $(9 + 5)^2 + (10 - 2)$

3) $(9 \times 2 + 4^2) + 4$

4) $(14 - 4)^2 + (18 - 3)$

5) $6 \times (11 + 5) - 9^2$

6) $(50 - 2) - 4 - 4^2$

7) $(53 - 3) - 2 + 2^2$

8) $(7 \times 4 - 4^2) - 10$

9) $(72 - 6^2) - (11 - 2)$

10) $4 \times (13 + 6) - 6^2$

1) $(13 \times 10 - 9^2) - 8$

2) $(8 - 2)^2 + (18 - 6)$

3) $(55 - 5) - 2 - 4^2$

4) $(72 - 6^2) - (-2 + 4)$

5) $(55 - 5) - 2 + 2^2$

6) $(44 - 4^2) - (-2 + 4)$

7) $(10 \times 7 + 2^2) - 3$

8) $3 \times (10 + 3) - 5^2$

9) $(6 + 3)^2 + (15 - 5)$

10) $3 \times (9 - 4) - 3^2$

Name:_____

Score:

_____

1) $(28 - 2^2) - (6 - 2)$

2) $4 \times (12 + 4) - 6^2$

3) $(3 \times 7 - 2^2) + 8$

4) $(41 - 5) - 3 - 3^2$

5) $8 \times (10 - 6) + 3^2$

6) $(3 \times 10 - 6^2) + 7$

7) $(61 - 5^2) - (-2 + 5)$

8) $(12 - 4)^2 + (12 - 6)$

9) $(8 - 2)^2 + (14 - 2)$

10) $(65 - 5) - 20 + 3^2$

| Day 27 | **Name**:_____ | Score:
_____ |

1) $(34 - 4) - 15 + 5^2$

2) $8 \times (9 - 5) + 8^2$

3) $(34 - 2) - 8 + 4^2$

4) $(55 - 5^2) - (13 - 3)$

5) $(9 + 2)^2 + (14 - 7)$

6) $(9 \times 8 - 3^2) + 2$

7) $(34 - 2^2) - (8 - 5)$

8) $7 \times (10 + 2) + 4^2$

9) $(10 \times 4 - 3^2) + 5$

10) $(7 + 2)^2 + (20 - 5)$

Name:_____

Score:
_____

1) $(34 - 4) - 15 + 5^2$

2) $8 \times (9 - 5) + 8^2$

3) $(34 - 2) - 8 + 4^2$

4) $(55 - 5^2) - (13 - 3)$

5) $(9 + 2)^2 + (14 - 7)$

6) $(9 \times 8 - 3^2) + 2$

7) $(34 - 2^2) - (8 - 5)$

8) $7 \times (10 + 2) + 4^2$

9) $(10 \times 4 - 3^2) + 5$

10) $(7 + 2)^2 + (20 - 5)$

1) $(5 \times 6 - 2^2) + 8$

2) $(42 - 2) - 10 - 4^2$

3) $(9 + 3)^2 + (15 - 3)$

4) $(36 - 4) - 2 - 2^2$

5) $(7 \times 7 + 3^2) + 6$

6) $(9 + 5)^2 + (18 - 6)$

7) $(52 - 4^2) - (1 + 2)$

8) $(96 - 6^2) - (19 - 4)$

9) $2 \times (12 - 5) - 5^2$

10) $8 \times (11 + 3) + 3^2$

1) $(35 - 5) - 10 - 4^2$

2) $(64 - 4) - 6 - 2^2$

3) $(7 \times 3 + 5^2) + 8$

4) $3 \times (9 + 2) - 4^2$

5) $(36 - 2^2) - (2 + 2)$

6) $(8 - 4)^2 + (18 - 2)$

7) $2 \times (11 + 5) + 6^2$

8) $(7 \times 6 + 7^2) + 4$

9) $(45 - 3^2) - (5 - 2)$

10) $(10 + 2)^2 + (20 - 4)$

1) ((10 + 3) x 5) - 4

6) (6 + (14 - 7 + 9))

2) (9 + (14 - 7)) x 5

7) 19 + (3 x (11 - 4))

3) (12 + (14 - 2)) x 4

8) (12 + (16 - 8 + 4))

4) ((18 - 3) + 7) + 13

9) 14 + ((16 - 3) + 2)

5) 15 + ((18 + 6) + 6)

10) 6 + (3 + (13 + 7))

1)   8 + ((9 - 3) x 6)

2) ((13 - 6) x 2) +12

3) (16 +(8 - 2)) x 4

4)   12 +(2 x (14 + 3))

5)   8 +(6 x (10 + 6))

6)   15 + ((10 + 3) x 4)

7) (11 +(8 - 2)) + 5

8) (4 +(20 - 4 + 8))

9) (8 +(20 - 4 - 7))

10) ((10 - 7) + 4) +12

1) 12 +(8 x (12 + 8))

2) ((15 +2) + 4) + 3

3) 15 + ((15 - 4) + 6)

4) 2 +(4 + (11 + 2))

5) 19 + ((16 + 7) + 6)

6) (13 + (18 - 2 + 2))

7) (18 +(8 - 2)) + 3

8) ((12 - 8) x 5) - 12

9) (16 + (12 - 6)) + 2

10) (9 + (15 - 3 - 3))

	Score:
Day 34	**Name**:_____

1)   9 + ((11 + 6) + 5)

2) (9 + (15 - 5)) x 5

3) (10 + (14 - 7 - 8))

4) (15 + (20 - 2)) x 6

5)   5 + (5 x (10 - 2))

6) ((13 - 5) x 4) + 11

7) (7 + (18 - 2 + 5))

8)   7 + ((17 + 2) x 2)

9) ((13 + 6) x 2) + 5

10)   3 + (9 x (9 + 5))

1) ((18 - 2) + 2) - 6

2) (6 +(12 - 6 + 9))

3) 18 +(7 x (10 - 3))

4) ((11 +4) + 6) - 5

5) (7 +(15 - 3 + 2))

6) (11 +(12 - 2)) + 4

7) 2 +(3 x (16 - 3))

8) (17 +(12 - 3)) x 7

9) 8 +((11 - 2) x 5)

10) 7 +((18 - 6) + 6)

| Day 36 | **Name**:_____ | **Score:**_____ |

1) (9 +(14 - 7 - 6))

2)   3 +(7 +(10 + 6))

3) (15 +(18 - 2)) + 2

4) ((14 - 4) + 6) + 6

5)   11 + ((18 - 4) x 5)

6) ((16 - 2) x 2) + 9

7)   8 + ((17 + 3) x 4)

8)   2 +(5 +(16 + 8))

9) (13 +(18 - 6 + 7))

10) (16 +(10 - 5)) + 4

1) $9 + (4 \times (14 + 2))$

2) $((18 - 6) \times 3) + 3$

3) $9 + ((12 - 5) \times 3)$

4) $(2 + (14 - 2 + 3))$

5) $(2 + (12 - 4 - 3))$

6) $(18 + (8 - 4)) + 5$

7) $((15 + 8) \times 6) - 3$

8) $6 + (9 + (12 - 7))$

9) $13 + ((14 - 3) \times 2)$

10) $(17 + (12 - 3)) \times 2$

1) 15 + (2 + (13 - 2))

6) 19 + ((15 - 3) + 6)

2) (5 + (14 - 2 - 7))

7) (17 + (14 - 2)) + 6

3) ((17 + 3) x 7) - 8

8) 16 + ((17 + 6) + 4)

4) (11 + (12 - 3)) x 4

9) (7 + (8 - 4 + 4))

5) ((14 + 5) x 2) + 10

10) 18 + (9 x (9 - 5))

1)   8 + ((12 - 3) + 4)

2)   15 + (4 + (14 + 5))

3) ((9 - 6) x 5) - 6

4) (10 + (15 - 3 + 2))

5) (17 + (10 - 5)) x 4

6)   7 + (3 x (17 - 6))

7) ((12 + 5) + 3) + 11

8) (9 + (16 - 4 - 2))

9)   9 + ((14 - 7) + 4)

10) (15 + (12 - 6)) + 5

1) (4 +(18 - 3 - 6))

2) ((9 +7) + 3) + 9

3) ((12 +5) x 7) + 5

4) (16 +(16 - 2)) + 3

5)   7 + ((15 + 3) x 6)

6) (15 +(15 - 3)) x 5

7)   5 +(8 x (15 + 5))

8)   18 + ((10 - 7) x 2)

9)   16 +(6 + (12 - 3))

10) (11 +(15 - 5 + 7))

Day 41	**Name:**_____ **Score:** _____

1) $((4 + 2)^2 \times 6) - 2^2$

6) $((9 - 2)^2 + 5) + 5^2$

2) $((12 - 3) + (8 - 4)^2)$

7) $(3^2 + (14 - 7 + 4^2))$

3) $((11 + 7) + (18 - 3)^2)$

8) $5 + (3 + (11 - 2)^2)$

4) $10 + ((9 - 3) \times 4^2)$

9) $12 + (2 + (11 - 6)^2)$

5) $(3^2 + (14 - 7 + 3^2))$

10) $16 + ((11 - 5) + 3^2)$

1) $14 + ((12 + 4) \times 3^2)$

6) $((11 - 7) + (15 - 5)^2)$

2) $5 + (6 \times (6 + 3)^2)$

7) $(7^2 + (20 - 2 + 2^2))$

3) $14 + ((9 + 2) + 6^2)$

8) $((14 + 5) + (10 - 5)^2)$

4) $((11 - 2)^2 \times 7) - 2^2$

9) $((10 - 5)^2 \times 3) - 2^2$

5) $(6^2 + (24 - 2 + 4^2))$

10) $9 + (8 \times (3 + 2)^2)$

1) $17 + (9 + (10 - 3)^2)$

6) $8 + ((13 + 7) + 5^2)$

2) $((10 - 4) + (12 - 2)^2)$

7) $((11 - 3)^2 \times 2) + 6^2$

3) $((6 + 4)^2 + 2) + 4^2$

8) $5 + (10 \times (9 - 5)^2)$

4) $(7^2 + (12 - 6 + 2^2))$

9) $(5^2 + (24 - 2 + 4^2))$

5) $14 + ((18 - 2) \times 4^2)$

10) $((12 + 4) + (12 - 6)^2)$

1) $((11 - 5)^2 \times 7) + 6^2$

6) $((10 - 2) + (18 - 6)^2)$

2) $18 + ((13 - 3) + 4^2)$

7) $14 + (4 \times (10 - 4)^2)$

3) $13 + (8 \times (9 - 5)^2)$

8) $((11 - 3)^2 + 5) + 4^2$

4) $(6^2 + (24 - 12 + 4^2))$

9) $16 + ((9 + 6) \times 5^2)$

5) $(3^2 + (8 - 4 + 3^2))$

10) $((12 - 4) + (24 - 3)^2)$

1) $12 + (5 \times (5 + 3)^2)$

2) $(3^2 + (18 - 2 + 4^2))$

3) $((11 - 2)^2 + 6) + 6^2$

4) $((11 - 7) + (15 - 3)^2)$

5) $24 + ((15 + 4) \times 2^2)$

6) $((12 - 7) + (15 - 5)^2)$

7) $2 + (8 \times (11 - 5)^2)$

8) $8 + ((12 + 2) \times 6^2)$

9) $(3^2 + (15 - 3 + 2^2))$

10) $((9 - 2)^2 \times 4) + 8^2$

1) $12 + ((18 + 7) + 6^2)$

2) $4 + (6 + (6 + 5)^2)$

3) $(3^2 + (15 - 3 + 4^2))$

4) $((3 + 2)^2 + 3) - 3^2$

5) $((16 + 7) + (8 - 2)^2)$

6) $((18 + 3) + (14 - 7)^2)$

7) $14 + (5 + (6 + 4)^2)$

8) $14 + ((12 - 2) + 5^2)$

9) $(7^2 + (14 - 2 + 5^2))$

10) $((10 - 5)^2 \times 7) + 3^2$

1) $((9 - 6)^2 \times 2) + 6^2$

2) $18 + ((15 + 4) \times 3^2)$

3) $13 + (8 + (11 - 5)^2)$

4) $((11 + 3) + (15 - 5)^2)$

5) $6 + (9 + (5 + 5)^2)$

6) $((3 + 2)^2 + 5) + 8^2$

7) $8 + ((11 - 6) \times 4^2)$

8) $(6^2 + (24 - 12 + 3^2))$

9) $(3^2 + (8 - 4 + 2^2))$

10) $((14 - 6) + (12 - 6)^2)$

1) $14 + (6 + (5 + 2)^2)$

2) $10 + ((18 + 4) + 3^2)$

3) $14 + ((15 - 3) \times 5^2)$

4) $((6 + 4)^2 + 6) - 4^2$

5) $19 + (9 + (9 - 5)^2)$

6) $((10 - 4) + (14 - 7)^2)$

7) $(3^2 + (24 - 3 + 2^2))$

8) $((11 - 4)^2 \times 7) - 4^2$

9) $((9 - 7) + (16 - 8)^2)$

10) $(6^2 + (10 - 2 + 3^2))$

1) $(4^2 + (12 - 3 + 3^2))$

2) $((11 + 4) + (8 - 2)^2)$

3) $((11 - 3)^2 \times 6) + 3^2$

4) $((12 - 4) + (16 - 2)^2)$

5) $(3^2 + (8 - 4 + 4^2))$

6) $14 + ((17 - 6) \times 3^2)$

7) $15 + ((9 + 3) + 3^2)$

8) $((5 + 4)^2 + 4) - 3^2$

9) $5 + (8 + (11 - 4)^2)$

10) $7 + (6 + (9 - 4)^2)$

1) $((5 + 2)^2 \times 3) - 2^2$

6) $24 + ((10 + 3) + 3^2)$

2) $((12 + 7) + (15 - 3)^2)$

7) $(5^2 + (8 - 2 + 3^2))$

3) $13 + (5 \times (6 + 3)^2)$

8) $((14 - 2) + (16 - 2)^2)$

4) $(5^2 + (10 - 5 + 3^2))$

9) $6 + (10 \times (4 + 6)^2)$

5) $20 + ((18 + 7) \times 5^2)$

10) $((5 + 3)^2 + 6) + 2^2$

Day 51	**Name**:_____	**Score:**

1) 14 - 3 x 7 + 16 - 8

2) 4 - 2 + 4 x 8 + 19

3) 5 x 14 + 10 x 16 + 9

4) 9 + 2 x 5 - 4 - 2

5) 6 x 7 x 2 - 1 - 1

6) 9 - 1 + 15 - 13 x 12

7) 18 x 6 + 18 + 19 x 4

8) 9 x 10 + 11 - 11 - 10

9) 19 + 10 - 6 - 4 x 17

10) 2 - 1 x 19 x 12 + 6

Day 52	**Name:** _____ **Score:** _____

1) 16 - 6 x 11 + 14 - 14

6) 11 x 16 x 2 - 1 + 3

2) 15 x 18 - 9 - 8 + 9

7) 8 + 10 - 8 x 2 x 7

3) 2 x 17 - 11 + 4 x 7

8) 5 x 11 - 9 x 3 + 7

4) 16 x 3 + 9 x 12 - 5

9) 14 x 12 - 4 - 1 + 5

5) 16 - 15 x 13 x 17 + 4

10) 4 - 3 - 1 x 2 + 15

1) 9 - 1 + 11 + 13 x 19

2) 2 - 1 + 13 x 19 + 7

3) 15 x 19 + 11 - 7 + 12

4) 10 - 7 x 4 + 3 - 2

5) 19 - 7 x 4 + 15 + 6

6) 12 + 11 x 4 - 3 - 1

7) 12 - 10 + 3 x 9 + 8

8) 13 + 5 x 17 - 12 + 4

9) 17 x 6 - 6 + 7 x 9

10) 13 x 14 - 11 + 5 x 11

1) 10 x 14 - 9 + 17 + 5

2) 2 + 3 + 7 - 2 x 14

3) 16 + 5 x 15 - 2 + 19

4) 8 - 5 + 3 x 16 x 8

5) 16 + 5 - 3 + 6 - 5

6) 2 + 4 - 3 - 1 x 2

7) 19 + 3 + 18 - 9 - 5

8) 13 x 13 - 3 x 8 + 8

9) 14 + 12 + 12 - 10 x 12

10) 17 - 3 x 7 + 6 + 9

1) $13 - 6 \times 19 + 5 - 3$

2) $3 + 10 + 12 - 11 \times 10$

3) $15 \times 15 - 13 + 3 + 19$

4) $8 \times 17 + 10 + 4 - 2$

5) $18 + 7 \times 7 - 4 - 4$

6) $5 - 3 + 15 - 9 + 7$

7) $19 - 15 \times 11 + 9 \times 7$

8) $13 - 5 + 5 + 10 \times 14$

9) $9 - 3 + 5 \times 11 - 10$

10) $5 + 8 - 2 \times 14 - 11$

Day 56	**Name:**_____	**Score:**_____

1) 2 + 13 - 2 x 10 + 2

2) 10 - 4 + 7 + 19 x 5

3) 8 + 2 x 12 x 14 - 10

4) 19 x 4 + 9 x 17 - 12

5) 5 - 1 + 11 + 5 x 5

6) 11 - 4 + 19 x 2 - 1

7) 14 x 4 x 9 - 2 + 5

8) 13 + 19 x 14 x 18 + 15

9) 19 + 4 x 2 - 1 + 18

10) 7 + 9 - 8 x 13 - 7

Day 57	**Name**:	**Score:**

1) 14 + 5 x 16 + 7 x 12

2) 12 + 2 x 17 - 16 x 14

3) 19 - 2 + 11 x 12 x 3

4) 7 + 7 - 4 x 9 x 18

5) 2 + 4 x 7 - 5 - 1

6) 12 x 19 - 7 + 11 x 10

7) 17 x 5 - 4 + 5 - 2

8) 7 x 16 + 8 + 9 x 11

9) 12 x 10 x 7 + 9 + 15

10) 13 - 6 + 6 - 1 x 14

Day 58	**Name**:_____	Score:_____

1) 3 + 15 - 4 x 18 - 5

2) 12 + 13 - 6 x 11 - 4

3) 5 - 2 + 5 + 10 - 6

4) 17 x 18 + 3 - 2 x 4

5) 7 x 10 - 10 + 8 - 3

6) 10 x 17 - 12 + 4 - 4

7) 10 - 4 + 15 - 10 x 13

8) 18 + 5 x 12 - 12 + 14

9) 7 + 7 + 12 - 6 x 14

10) 3 + 16 - 2 x 13 - 3

1) 16 - 4 x 13 x 18 + 13

2) 11 - 5 x 5 - 4 + 9

3) 6 x 2 x 4 + 2 + 16

4) 11 + 8 - 6 + 15 x 17

5) 3 + 4 - 1 + 10 x 11

6) 6 x 7 + 11 x 19 - 17

7) 17 x 2 + 13 + 12 x 15

8) 9 - 2 - 1 x 12 + 14

9) 7 - 5 + 3 x 3 + 8

10) 19 - 13 + 17 - 11 x 14

1) $16 - 12 + 15 + 19 \times 4$

2) $6 - 2 + 10 \times 16 - 7$

3) $16 + 6 \times 13 \times 9 - 6$

4) $2 + 15 - 5 \times 11 - 5$

5) $6 + 6 - 4 \times 8 \times 9$

6) $18 + 16 + 6 \times 14 - 2$

7) $4 \times 13 \times 18 + 19 - 4$

8) $14 \times 6 - 3 - 1 + 15$

9) $9 + 13 - 3 + 14 \times 13$

10) $9 - 9 + 18 \times 5 - 2$

Day 61	**Name:**	**Score:**

1) (10 - 5) x (12 + 4) + 4

6) (17 - 3) x (14 + 4) + 10

2) (9 + 45 - 4) + 5 + 7

7)   7 x (11 x 4 + 10) - 3

3) (10 + 35 - 5) - (15 - 5)

8) (14 - 2) x (6 + 12 - 3)

4) (12 - 5) x (10 + 10 - 5)

9)   5 x (2 x 6 + 9) - 9

5) (14 + 20 - 6) + 4 + 7

10) (12 + 17 - 5) - (2 + 2)

| Day 62 | **Name:**_____ | Score:_____ |

1) (8 + 4) x (10 + 15 - 3)

2) (8 + 45 - 3) - (27 - 2)

3) (21 - 3) x (13 + 6) - 7

4) (8 + 42 - 2) + 6 + 2

5) (10 - 3) x (6 + 10 - 2)

6) 2 x (13 x 9 + 5) - 8

7) (10 + 43 - 3) - (27 - 2)

8) 2 x (13 x 8 - 8) + 6

9) (14 + 19 - 5) + 2 + 4

10) (10 - 7) x (12 + 6) - 3

Day 63

Name:_____

Score:
_____

1) (9 +21 - 6) + 6 + 5

2) (8 +29 - 5) - (2 + 6)

3) (13 + 4) x (12 + 6) + 8

4)   8 x (6 x 10 + 8) +10

5)   7 x (8 x   9 - 10) +10

6) (14 +40 - 6) - (-3 + 6)

7) (14 -   4) x (10 +12 - 4)

8) (14 -   3) x (7 +10 - 5)

9) (12 +24 - 4) +16 + 2

10) (14 + 2) x (13 - 2) - 7

1) (10 + 31 - 5) + 18 - 3

2) (9 + 43 - 4) - (6 + 2)

3) (9 + 32 - 5) - (1 + 3)

4) (10 + 6) x (9 - 6) + 9

5) (13 - 5) x (8 + 4) - 5

6) (15 + 2) x (9 + 12 - 2)

7) (14 + 37 - 3) + 12 + 4

8) 10 x (10 x 5 - 4) + 8

9) 4 x (7 x 6 - 7) + 5

10) (15 - 3) x (14 + 10 - 5)

Day 65	**Name:** _____

Score: _____

1) $(16 - 2) \times (7 + 12 - 6)$

2) $4 \times (11 \times 2 - 8) + 7$

3) $(15 + 21 - 6) + 2 - 5$

4) $(8 + 33 - 5) + 6 - 3$

5) $(16 + 5) \times (10 + 18 - 9)$

6) $(14 + 28 - 2) - (16 + 4)$

7) $(17 - 5) \times (8 + 4) - 3$

8) $(20 + 8) \times (8 + 6) + 10$

9) $7 \times (9 \times 5 + 7) - 5$

10) $(10 + 34 - 4) - (10 - 2)$

1) $(14 + 5) \times (12 + 2) + 6$

2) $7 \times (5 \times 6 - 7) + 4$

3) $(16 - 6) \times (11 + 6) - 10$

4) $5 \times (6 \times 5 + 5) - 6$

5) $(14 + 19 - 3) - (6 - 3)$

6) $(8 - 4) \times (13 + 18 - 6)$

7) $(14 + 21 - 5) + 2 - 7$

8) $(8 - 4) \times (11 + 24 - 2)$

9) $(11 + 26 - 5) + 8 + 3$

10) $(10 + 26 - 6) - (-3 + 6)$

Name:_____

Score:
_____

1) (14 + 22 - 6) + 2 + 6

6) (9 + 26 - 5) - (5 - 2)

2) (16 + 5) x (6 + 16 - 2)

7) 8 x (13 x 8 + 3) + 7

3) (12 + 21 - 5) - (-1 + 3)

8) (11 + 2) x (6 + 18 - 3)

4) 3 x (11 x 10 + 9) + 10

9) (11 + 31 - 6) + 2 + 5

5) (13 - 4) x (9 + 2) - 8

10) (15 - 4) x (9 + 6) - 10

1) (16 + 5) x (9 + 2) - 2

2) (11 - 2) x (10 - 2) + 10

3)   5 x (13 x 6 - 3) + 2

4) (13 + 41 - 4) - (2 + 3)

5)   6 x (4 x 2 + 9) + 10

6) (13 + 4) x (8 + 15 - 3)

7) (15 + 17 - 4) + 2 + 7

8) (15 + 31 - 6) - (1 + 7)

9) (14 + 32 - 6) + 20 + 6

10) (13 - 3) x (11 + 10 - 5)

1) (20 + 4) x (8 - 2) - 3

2) (13 +52 - 5) - (-1 + 6)

3) (9 - 3) x (14 +18 - 2)

4) (10 +44 - 6) - (-1 + 4)

5) (9 + 5) x (9 +24 - 6)

6) (16 - 3) x (12 + 2) +10

7) (13 +29 - 6) + 3 + 2

8) (14 +31 - 5) + 5 - 3

9) 5 x (3 x 10 - 4) - 9

10) 9 x (11 x 9 - 6) +10

1) (10 + 42 - 2) + 25 + 7

6)   2 x (10 x 7 - 4) - 6

2) (15 + 4) x (15 + 8 - 4)

7) (9 + 22 - 3) - (-4 + 6)

3) (11 + 52 - 3) + 5 - 5

8) (10 + 41 - 3) - (14 - 2)

4)   3 x (7 x 3 + 8) - 10

9) (10 + 4) x (11 + 5) - 7

5) (17 + 2) x (12 + 3) - 4

10) (13 + 5) x (9 + 10 - 2)

1) $8 \times (6 \times 4 - 6^2) - 8$

2) $(14 + 19 - 3) - 15 - 2^2$

3) $(12 + 31 - 3) - 10 - 4^2$

4) $(6 + 4)^2 + (12 + 18 + 9)$

5) $(19 - 7) \times (11 - 5) + 2^2$

6) $(14 + 46 - 6^2) + (5 - 2)$

7) $(17 + 6) \times (8 - 3) + 9^2$

8) $(14 - 5)^2 + (16 + 10 + 2)$

9) $4 \times (8 \times 10 + 7^2) - 3$

10) $(10 + 65 - 5^2) + (8 - 6)$

1) $(17 + 2) \times (12 + 6) - 6^2$

2) $(6 + 2)^2 + (13 + 10 - 5)$

3) $5 \times (3 \times 7 + 2^2) + 10$

4) $(13 + 18 - 3) - 4 + 4^2$

5) $(12 + 40 - 2^2) + (1 + 7)$

6) $(10 + 5)^2 + (15 + 12 + 4)$

7) $(9 + 44 - 5^2) + (1 + 6)$

8) $9 \times (13 \times 2 + 4^2) + 10$

9) $(11 + 42 - 5) - 3 - 5^2$

10) $(20 + 2) \times (12 - 3) - 3^2$

1) $(15 + 17 - 2) - 10 + 3^2$

2) $4 \times (11 \times 5 + 7^2) + 3$

3) $(12 + 38 - 2) - 8 + 6^2$

4) $(17 + 6) \times (13 + 6) - 9^2$

5) $(16 - 7) \times (13 + 6) - 9^2$

6) $(13 + 41 - 2^2) + (12 - 2)$

7) $(2 + 3)^2 + (12 + 20 - 4)$

8) $(5 + 4)^2 + (15 + 12 - 6)$

9) $(11 + 53 - 6^2) + (3 + 4)$

10) $2 \times (10 \times 6 - 2^2) + 5$

Day 74	Name:_____	Score: _____

1) $(15 + 40 - 5^2) + (4 + 6)$

6) $(13 - 5)^2 + (15 + 12 + 3)$

2) $(10 + 3)^2 + (12 + 8 - 4)$

7) $(15 + 38 - 3) - 5 + 2^2$

3) $7 \times (13 \times 10 - 4^2) + 9$

8) $(10 + 32 - 6) - 9 - 7^2$

4) $(15 + 33 - 4^2) + (19 - 3)$

9) $(14 + 2) \times (12 - 4) - 2^2$

5) $(20 - 3) \times (14 + 5) - 5^2$

10) $7 \times (4 \times 10 + 4^2) - 3$

| Day 75 | Name:_____ | Score:_____ |

1) $(21 + 3) \times (14 - 4) - 4^2$

2) $6 \times (13 \times 9 + 8^2) - 6$

3) $(11 - 2) \times (10 - 6) + 2^2$

4) $3 \times (6 \times 6 + 8^2) - 5$

5) $(13 - 2)^2 + (9 + 10 + 5)$

6) $(14 + 61 - 5^2) + (4 - 2)$

7) $(3 + 4)^2 + (16 + 20 + 5)$

8) $(9 + 18 - 3) - 12 - 2^2$

9) $(10 + 18 - 4) - 2 + 3^2$

10) $(9 + 35 - 2^2) + (2 + 6)$

1) $(12 + 3) \times (11 - 4) - 5^2$

2) $(9 - 4)^2 + (7 + 16 + 2)$

3) $(11 - 3) \times (11 + 6) + 8^2$

4) $(10 - 4)^2 + (9 + 18 + 9)$

5) $8 \times (11 \times 3 + 3^2) + 8$

6) $(15 + 20 - 5) - 2 - 2^2$

7) $(11 + 26 - 3^2) + (3 + 4)$

8) $6 \times (13 \times 5 - 6^2) - 10$

9) $(9 + 48 - 5^2) + (3 + 5)$

10) $(10 + 23 - 5) - 7 - 3^2$

1) $(14 - 4) \times (10 + 2) + 2^2$

2) $(10 + 55 - 5) - 6 + 6^2$

3) $(8 + 20 - 2^2) + (1 + 3)$

4) $(12 - 3)^2 + (12 + 24 + 12)$

5) $(9 + 60 - 3^2) + (35 - 5)$

6) $(11 - 6) \times (13 - 3) + 6^2$

7) $8 \times (12 \times 10 + 8^2) - 8$

8) $4 \times (3 \times 9 - 6^2) - 4$

9) $(6 + 4)^2 + (13 + 15 - 3)$

10) $(12 + 30 - 6) - 12 + 6^2$

1) $8 \times (2 \times 6 + 7^2) - 7$

6) $(18 - 8) \times (9 + 6) - 4^2$

2) $(11 + 39 - 2) - 24 + 4^2$

7) $(7 + 4)^2 + (5 + 24 - 6)$

3) $(20 - 5) \times (10 + 3) - 5^2$

8) $(12 + 34 - 6) - 8 - 5^2$

4) $(3 + 4)^2 + (11 + 8 + 4)$

9) $(10 + 30 - 4^2) + (-3 + 5)$

5) $(12 + 54 - 6^2) + (8 - 5)$

10) $4 \times (7 \times 8 + 6^2) - 7$

Day 79	**Name**:_____	**Score:** _____

1) $3 \times (3 \times 10 + 4^2) - 3$

2) $(15 + 6) \times (10 - 5) - 3^2$

3) $(12 + 27 - 3^2) + (11 + 4)$

4) $(9 - 2)^2 + (6 + 10 + 5)$

5) $7 \times (9 \times 8 - 4^2) - 10$

6) $(12 + 21 - 3) - 6 - 5^2$

7) $(9 + 25 - 2^2) + (8 - 2)$

8) $(9 + 3)^2 + (10 + 14 - 7)$

9) $(21 - 8) \times (14 + 3) - 4^2$

10) $(13 + 16 - 5) - 3 + 2^2$

1) $9 \times (13 \times 8 + 5^2) + 2$

6) $(20 - 5) \times (11 + 6) - 8^2$

2) $(8 + 27 - 5) - 6 - 6^2$

7) $(8 + 4)^2 + (6 + 14 + 7)$

3) $(12 + 18 - 2) - 7 - 3^2$

8) $3 \times (9 \times 7 + 7^2) + 10$

4) $(14 - 2) \times (13 + 2) - 3^2$

9) $(10 + 24 - 2^2) + (4 - 2)$

5) $(10 - 3)^2 + (11 + 18 - 3)$

10) $(12 + 54 - 6^2) + (7 - 5)$

1) (5 +(15 + 3 - 4)) + 5

6) 16 +(8 + (18 - 2)) - 3

2) ((12 - 5) + 6) + 5 + 3

7) ((15 - 5) +(14 - 2)) x 5

3) (10 - 5)+ ((10 - 4) x 2)

8) (13 +(20 + 4 + 6)) - 4

4) ((18 + 6) - (14 - 2)) + 7

9) 19 +(7 x (14 + 6)) + 4

5) ((10 - 3) + 3) - 2 - 3

10) (12 - 2)+ ((11 - 4) + 2)

1) ((9 + 5) - (24 - 4)) x 7

6) ((12 - 7) x 6) + 9 - 10

2) (2 +(10 + 2 - 5)) - 2

7)   9 +(3 + (12 + 6)) + 7

3) (16 - 2) + ((15 + 3) x 5)

8) (12 - 3) + ((14 - 4) x 3)

4) ((12 - 2) - (15 - 5)) x 3

9)   4 +(4 x (10 + 4)) - 8

5) ((11 - 4) + 4) - 4 + 3

10) (8 +(10 + 5 + 8)) - 9

Day 83	**Name**:	**Score:**

1)   9 +(4 x (13 - 7)) + 3

2) ((11 - 2) +(20 - 4)) x 5

3) (24 -   6) + ((17 - 2) x 5)

4) ((10 - 3) + 6) +12 +10

5) (10 +(24 + 2 - 9)) + 6

6)   19 +(6 + (17 + 4)) - 4

7) ((12 - 5) x 5) + 4 - 10

8) ((10 - 5) +(12 - 3)) x 2

9) (10 +(14 + 7 - 9)) + 5

10) (10 -   5) + ((12 + 5) x 2)

Day 84

Name:_____

Score:_____

1) (2 +(20 + 2 + 2)) - 6

2) (10 - 2) + ((17 - 7) x 5)

3) ((17 - 6) + 7) + 4 - 4

4) (10 - 2) + ((10 + 3) + 4)

5)   2 +(8 +(14 - 6)) + 7

6) (11 +(12 + 4 + 3)) - 3

7) ((9 + 5) - (15 - 5)) + 7

8) ((18 + 2) - (20 - 10)) + 7

9)   17 +(6 x (17 - 3)) - 3

10) ((16 + 2) x 3) - 6 - 9

1) ((12 - 4) x 5) +10 - 9

6) 9 +(2 +(9 - 3)) +10

2) (8 +(12 + 3 + 6)) - 3

7) ((17 + 7) - (24 - 6)) + 4

3) (16 - 4) + ((11 + 7) + 4)

8) ((18 - 4) + 4) + 5 - 3

4) (18 - 9) + ((11 - 7) x 5)

9) 14 +(4 +(15 - 8)) + 3

5) ((16 + 3) +(8 - 4)) x 3

10) (9 +(12 + 3 - 5)) - 2

Day 86	**Name**:_____	Score:_____

1)   15 + (6 + (10 + 4)) - 9

2) (12 -   3) + ((9 + 3) x 5)

3) ((10 + 4) - (18 - 6)) x 7

4) ((10 - 4) + (24 - 8)) + 2

5) (4 + (18 + 6 - 5)) - 5

6) ((18 - 4) x 6) + 4 - 8

7) (7 + (12 + 2 - 7)) + 7

8) (16 -   8) + ((18 - 4) x 2)

9) ((17 + 2) x 4) - 8 - 7

10)   12 + (9 x (13 + 6)) - 3

1) (6 +(18 + 6 - 5)) + 5

2) ((14 +5) + 5) - 10 + 3

3) ((14 - 2) - (20 - 10)) x 2

4) ((10 - 5) x 4) + 3 + 8

5) (16 -   2) + ((14 - 7) x 6)

6) ((18 - 3) - (8 - 2)) + 6

7)   13 +(10 x (14 - 3)) +10

8) (7 +(15 + 3 - 2)) - 2

9) (15 -   3) + ((15 - 7) x 6)

10)   10 +(10 + (16 - 7)) - 6

1)   19 + (10 + (17 + 4)) + 2

2) (12 - 4) + ((14 - 4) x 5)

3) ((18 - 5) + 7) + 12 - 4

4) (20 - 4) + ((13 - 2) + 4)

5) (2 + (24 + 8 + 6)) - 8

6) ((16 + 7) - (10 - 2)) x 3

7)   3 + (5 x (12 + 2)) + 6

8) ((11 - 6) - (15 - 3)) + 2

9) (10 + (18 + 6 - 2)) + 7

10) ((13 - 7) x 5) - 12 + 3

1) (6 +(16 + 2 - 8)) - 8

2) (2 +(15 + 5 - 3)) - 2

3)   15 +(2 x (15 + 3)) - 4

4) (16 - 8) + ((10 + 3) x 6)

5)   13 +(3 x (10 - 2)) + 7

6) ((11 - 8) + 4) + 8 + 7

7) ((10 + 4) +(8 - 2)) x 5

8) (18 - 3) + ((14 + 2) + 6)

9) ((9 +6) x 5) - 11 +10

10) ((13 + 7) - (18 - 2)) + 2

1) (2 +(8 + 2 - 5)) + 7

2) (8 - 2) + ((13 - 6) x 3)

3)   5 +(8 x (17 + 2)) - 10

4) ((13 - 3) - (24 - 2)) + 7

5) ((15 + 6) +(8 - 2)) x 4

6) ((13 +6) x 3) + 4 - 4

7)   2 +(6 x (10 - 8)) + 9

8) (15 - 3) + ((15 + 7) x 5)

9) ((12 +5) + 6) + 9 - 7

10) (11 +(10 + 2 + 2)) + 5

Name:_____

Score:
_____

1) $(16 - 2)^2 + ((18 + 3) \times 2^2)$

2) $((17 + 7) + (12 - 4)^2) \times 6^2$

3) $(10 - 2)^2 + ((13 - 2) \times 5^2)$

4) $(4^2 + (16 - 2 + 5^2)) + 5^2$

5) $6 + (8 \times (10 - 2)^2) - 7$

6) $(5^2 + (12 - 3 + 2^2)) + 2^2$

7) $((11 - 4)^2 + 2) - 6 + 7^2$

8) $((17 + 2) + (15 - 5)^2) + 2^2$

9) $3 + (2 + (10 - 6)^2) + 9$

10) $((3 + 2)^2 \times 4) - 12 - 3^2$

Day 92	**Name**:_____	**Score:** _____

1) $(18 - 3)^2 + ((10 - 6) + 4^2)$

6) $((6 + 2)^2 + 7) - 9 - 2^2$

2) $((11 + 6) + (18 - 6)^2) \times 6^2$

7) $(7^2 + (20 - 10 + 5^2)) - 5^2$

3) $(12 - 6)^2 + ((16 + 5) \times 2^2)$

8) $(4^2 + (10 - 2 + 4^2)) - 5^2$

4) $2 + (2 \times (6 + 5)^2) - 8$

9) $((9 - 5)^2 \times 4) - 10 + 3^2$

5) $8 + (2 \times (9 - 6)^2) - 2$

10) $((16 - 3) + (8 - 4)^2) + 5^2$

Name:_____

Score:
_____

1) $(20 - 5)^2 + ((12 + 3) + 3^2)$

2) $((3 + 5)^2 \times 6) - 12 + 4^2$

3) $(3^2 + (16 - 2 + 4^2)) - 4^2$

4) $6 + (2 \times (4 + 4)^2) - 5$

5) $(8 - 4)^2 + ((11 - 5) \times 3^2)$

6) $(5^2 + (16 - 8 + 5^2)) - 2^2$

7) $13 + (5 \times (9 - 4)^2) + 3$

8) $((10 - 6)^2 \times 6) + 10 - 4^2$

9) $((15 + 7) + (16 - 8)^2) + 4^2$

10) $((11 - 7) + (10 - 5)^2) \times 2^2$

1) $((10 - 6)^2 \times 6) - 8 + 4^2$

6) $((9 - 2) + (16 - 4)^2) + 6^2$

2) $(15 - 3)^2 + ((12 + 6) \times 6^2)$

7) $4 + (6 \times (11 - 6)^2) - 7$

3) $(15 - 5)^2 + ((14 - 5) \times 6^2)$

8) $((4 + 4)^2 + 3) - 5 - 2^2$

4) $((13 - 2) + (18 - 9)^2) \times 7^2$

9) $2 + (2 \times (5 + 6)^2) - 6$

5) $(6^2 + (14 - 2 + 4^2)) + 2^2$

10) $(5^2 + (18 - 3 + 2^2)) + 2^2$

1) $(8 - 2)^2 + ((15 - 4) + 3^2)$

6) $((11 - 4)^2 \times 5) - 8 + 2^2$

2) $16 + (9 + (3 + 2)^2) + 8$

7) $((6 + 3)^2 \times 5) + 4 - 4^2$

3) $(7^2 + (10 - 2 + 4^2)) - 2^2$

8) $(3^2 + (14 - 7 + 3^2)) - 5^2$

4) $(12 - 2)^2 + ((12 - 5) \times 6^2)$

9) $((12 + 7) + (10 - 5)^2) \times 3^2$

5) $13 + (3 \times (3 + 4)^2) + 4$

10) $((9 - 3) + (18 - 2)^2) \times 7^2$

1) $10 + (7 \times (4 + 5)^2) + 8$

6) $((9 - 5)^2 \times 4) - 7 + 5^2$

2) $((17 - 2) + (16 - 4)^2) \times 2^2$

7) $((14 + 3) + (12 - 3)^2) \times 3^2$

3) $((11 - 4)^2 + 5) - 8 - 2^2$

8) $(4^2 + (18 - 3 + 5^2)) + 3^2$

4) $(14 - 7)^2 + ((17 - 5) + 5^2)$

9) $17 + (8 + (11 - 2)^2) + 8$

5) $(16 - 4)^2 + ((11 - 4) + 4^2)$

10) $(7^2 + (12 - 4 + 5^2)) - 4^2$

Day 97	Name:_____	Score: _____

1) $2 +(5 +(11 - 2)^2) - 8$

6) $((17 - 6) +(12 - 3)^2) \times 6^2$

2) $((11 + 3) +(8 - 4)^2) \times 4^2$

7) $(7^2 + (20 - 2 + 3^2)) + 4^2$

3) $((6 +2)^2 + 4) + 9 - 2^2$

8) $(8 - 2)^2 + ((18 - 4) + 5^2)$

4) $(7^2 + (14 - 2 + 2^2)) - 5^2$

9) $18 +(8 \times (4 + 3)^2) + 7$

5) $((4 +4)^2 \times 2) + 5 - 2^2$

10) $(24 - 8)^2 + ((12 + 3) + 4^2)$

1) $16 + (5 + (11 - 2)^2) + 8$

6) $(24 - 4)^2 + ((17 + 7) \times 2^2)$

2) $((9 - 3) + (8 - 4)^2) \times 6^2$

7) $((13 + 7) + (16 - 4)^2) \times 2^2$

3) $4 + (9 \times (10 - 4)^2) + 6$

8) $((9 - 2)^2 + 7) + 5 - 2^2$

4) $(5^2 + (16 - 4 + 4^2)) - 4^2$

9) $(15 - 3)^2 + ((17 + 7) + 5^2)$

5) $((11 - 4)^2 \times 3) + 6 - 4^2$

10) $(3^2 + (10 - 5 + 3^2)) + 4^2$

Day 99	**Name:** _____	**Score:** _____

1) $(3^2 + (15 - 5 + 4^2)) + 3^2$

2) $9 + (2 + (9 - 5)^2) - 8$

3) $(18 - 9)^2 + ((16 - 7) \times 3^2)$

4) $((4 + 3)^2 \times 6) - 10 - 4^2$

5) $14 + (2 + (4 + 2)^2) - 4$

6) $(5^2 + (18 - 2 + 4^2)) + 3^2$

7) $((14 + 5) + (10 - 2)^2) + 2^2$

8) $((11 - 3)^2 + 6) + 13 + 3^2$

9) $((15 - 5) + (18 - 2)^2) \times 4^2$

10) $(8 - 2)^2 + ((14 + 2) \times 5^2)$

Day 100	**Name**:_____	**Score:** _____

1) $7 + (5 \times (11 - 3)^2) - 7$

6) $((4 + 3)^2 \times 2) - 8 + 5^2$

2) $(16 - 8)^2 + ((15 - 4) + 3^2)$

7) $(3^2 + (8 - 4 + 4^2)) - 2^2$

3) $(20 - 5)^2 + ((9 - 3) + 4^2)$

8) $((17 + 7) + (12 - 3)^2) \times 5^2$

4) $((16 + 4) + (10 - 5)^2) \times 6^2$

9) $(3^2 + (24 - 2 + 4^2)) + 3^2$

5) $7 + (6 + (5 + 3)^2) - 5$

10) $((5 + 3)^2 + 7) - 10 + 6^2$

Answer Key

Day 1

1) 12 + 16 - 9 + 17
            36

2) 3 - 1 x 4 + 2
     3 -   4 + 2
              1

3) 11 + 11 x 3 + 5
    11 +   33 + 5
              49

4) 5 x 9 + 5 + 14
     45 + 5 + 14
           64

5) 14 + 19 x 6 + 19
    14 +   114 + 19
              147

6) 14 x 9 + 5 + 18
    126 + 5 + 18
           149

7) 9 + 2 x 3 + 17
     9 +   6 + 17
              32

8) 4 + 18 x 2 + 6
     4 +   36 + 6
               46

9) 7 + 18 x 8 - 2
     7 +   144 - 2
               149

10) 3 x 17 + 9 + 13
      51 + 9 + 13
            73

Day 2

1) 2 + 18 - 10 x 9
    2 + 18 -   90
                -70

2) 18 - 15 x 11 + 13
    18 -   165 + 13
                -134

3) 9 x 6 - 6 + 7
    54 - 6 + 7
           55

4) 2 + 6 - 1 + 9
           16

5) 18 x 19 + 3 + 15
    342 + 3 + 15
           360

6) 5 + 7 x 17 - 10
    5 +   119 - 10
              114

7) 5 + 8 x 10 + 15
    5 +   80 + 15
              100

8) 9 x 4 - 2 + 17
    36 - 2 + 17
           51

9) 4 + 10 x 17 - 5
    4 +   170 - 5
              169

10) 8 x 18 + 16 + 8
     144 + 16 + 8
              168

Day 3

1) 18 - 13 + 6 + 13
                  24

2) 16 + 6 + 11 - 2
                  31

3) 6 + 12 - 12 x 7
    6 + 12 -   84
              -66

4) 12 + 9 + 6 - 5
                  22

5) 3 + 11 x 10 + 10
    3 +   110 + 10
                  123

6) 16 - 15 + 12 + 2
                  15

7) 18 + 14 - 6 + 10
                  36

8) 2 + 8 + 19 - 13
                  16

9) 8 + 6 - 3 x 19
    8 + 6 -   57
                  -43

10) 17 x 12 + 16 - 5
     204 + 16 - 5
                  215

Day 4

1) 19 x 19 + 15 + 2
361 + 15 + 2
378

2) 9 - 3 x 13 + 12
9 - 39 + 12
-18

3) 13 x 18 + 4 + 7
234 + 4 + 7
245

4) 17 - 12 + 5 + 13
23

5) 17 + 12 + 16 - 10
35

6) 14 + 4 x 9 - 9
14 + 36 - 9
41

7) 14 - 3 + 12 x 10
14 - 3 + 120
131

8) 12 + 5 + 8 x 12
12 + 5 + 96
113

9) 16 x 15 - 4 + 3
240 - 4 + 3
239

10) 14 + 4 + 11 x 5
14 + 4 + 55
73

Day 5

1) 9 + 8 x 2 +12
    9 +   16 + 12
           37

2) 13 + 6 x 10 +12
    13 +   60 + 12
         85

3) 4 x 4 - 1 +16
    16 - 1 + 16
       31

4) 2 - 1 + 8 + 6
     15

5) 4 x 3 +15 +11
    12 + 15 + 11
      38

6) 2 - 1 +11 + 9
        21

7) 14 x 19 + 6 + 17
    266 + 6 + 17
       289

8) 2 +13 - 2 x 8
   2 + 13 -   16
         -1

9) 15 +19 + 5 - 1
      38

10) 5 + 4 - 3 + 3
     9

Day 6

1) 16 - 14 + 13 x 7
    16 - 14 +   91
              93

2) 2 - 1 + 19 + 18
             38

3) 9 x 8 + 4 + 19
    72 + 4 + 19
          95

4) 13 x 17 + 19 - 18
    221 + 19 - 18
         222

5) 5 + 12 x 18 + 13
    5 +   216 + 13
        234

6) 12 + 11 - 8 + 11
           26

7) 16 + 7 + 7 - 3
           27

8) 8 - 5 x 6 + 17
    8 -   30 + 17
         -5

9) 14 - 3 + 12 + 2
           25

10) 17 + 19 + 17 x 11
    17 + 19 +   187
         223

Day 7

1) $10 + 12 \times 17 + 17$
    $10 + \quad 204 + 17$
             231

2) $19 + 18 + 2 - 1$
            38

3) $18 - 11 \times 17 + 2$
    $18 - \quad 187 + 2$
            -167

4) $4 \times 11 + 2 + 5$
     $44 + 2 + 5$
         51

5) $15 + 17 - 12 \times 6$
   $15 + 17 - \quad 72$
         -40

6) $2 + 11 - 5 + 10$
           18

7) $15 \times 16 + 16 + 12$
    $240 + 16 + 12$
         268

8) $8 + 16 + 18 \times 16$
   $8 + 16 + \quad 288$
         312

9) $12 - 6 + 16 + 3$
         25

10) $3 - 2 \times 16 + 17$
   $3 - \quad 32 + 17$
        -12

Day 8

1) 11 - 8 x 10 + 12
    11 -   80 + 12
            -57

2) 5 - 1 + 12 + 16
           32

3) 5 - 3 + 15 x 5
    5 - 3 +   75
          77

4) 8 x 9 + 3 - 3
    72 + 3 - 3
          72

5) 18 + 3 + 2 - 1
        22

6) 16 x 8 + 7 + 17
    128 + 7 + 17
          152

7) 14 + 15 x 7 - 5
    14 +   105 - 5
          114

8) 13 + 7 + 5 x 9
    13 + 7 +   45
          65

9) 7 + 18 - 5 x 19
    7 + 18 -   95
          -70

10) 19 x 13 - 7 + 6
    247 - 7 + 6
          246

Day 9

1) 15 + 2 - 1 x 11
    15 + 2 -   11
            6

2) 15 - 13 + 8 x 5
    15 - 13 +   40
            42

3) 11 + 18 - 5 x 18
    11 + 18 -   90
          -61

4) 2 + 17 x 16 + 14
    2 +   272 + 14
        288

5) 3 + 18 + 19 - 19
        21

6) 18 x 8 - 3 + 12
    144 - 3 + 12
        153

7) 10 - 3 x 8 + 13
    10 -   24 + 13
        -1

8) 8 x 12 + 6 - 2
    96 + 6 - 2
       100

9) 6 x 17 - 13 + 13
    102 - 13 + 13
       102

10) 4 - 2 x 18 + 3
    4 -   36 + 3
       -29

Day 10

1) 13 x 12 - 1 + 14
       156 - 1 + 14
             169

2) 14 - 6 x 3 + 15
     14 - 18 + 15
           11

3) 19 - 12 + 18 + 11
           36

4) 7 - 6 x 9 + 10
    7 - 54 + 10
         -37

5) 6 - 5 + 9 x 7
    6 - 5 + 63
        64

6) 8 + 17 + 11 - 6
          30

7) 9 + 15 + 3 x 10
   9 + 15 + 30
         54

8) 2 + 18 x 13 - 8
   2 + 234 - 8
        228

9) 15 x 5 + 7 - 3
    75 + 7 - 3
        79

10) 15 + 11 x 18 - 16
    15 + 198 - 16
        197

Day 11

1) $(17 + 4) \times 8 + 6$
      21     $\times$ 8 + 6
         168   + 6
             174

2) $10 \times 8 + (7 - 7)$
    $10 \times 8 +$ 0
     80   +   0
            80

3) $(9 + 5) + 15 \times 3$
     14   + 15 $\times$ 3
     14   +   45
           59

4) $(12 + 25 - 5) \times 16$
  (37   - 5) $\times$ 16
      32     $\times$ 16
       512

5) $(14 + 6) \times (7 + 5)$
    20    $\times$ 12
       240

6) $(11 + 3) \times 10 + 4$
     14     $\times$ 10 + 4
        140   + 4
         144

7) $4 \times 5 + (6 + 5)$
    $4 \times 5 +$ 11
     20   +   11
         31

8) $(16 + 3) + 16 \times 2$
     19   + 16 $\times$ 2
     19   +   32
         51

9) $(12 + 23 - 3) \times 16$
  (35   - 3) $\times$ 16
      32     $\times$ 16
       512

10) $(12 + 7) \times (13 + 2)$
    19    $\times$ 15
       285

Day 12

1) (15 - 8) x 14 + 2
    7   x 14 + 2
        98   + 2
              100

2) 6 x 4 +(8 - 5)
     6 x 4 +   3
        24   +   3
              27

3) (12 - 5)+ 10 x 2
     7   + 10 x 2
     7   +   20
              27

4) (13 +33 - 6) x 8
   (46   - 6) x 8
        40   x 8
              320

5) (11 + 2) x(7 - 3)
     13   x   4
              52

6) (14 + 5) x 8 - 5
     19   x 8 - 5
        152   - 5
              147

7) 7 x 11 +(6 + 7)
     7 x 11 +   13
        77   +   13
              90

8) (16 - 3)+ 14 x 7
     13   + 14 x 7
     13   +   98
              111

9) (14 +48 - 2) x 3
   (62   - 2) x 3
        60   x 3
              180

10) (11 + 3) x(8 - 2)
     14   x   6
              84

Day 13

1) $(16 - 7) \times 9 + 4$

   9 x 9 + 4

    81 + 4

      85

2) $7 \times 4 + (8 - 8)$

  7 x 4 + 0

   28 + 0

     28

3) $(9 + 5) + 20 \times 2$

   14 + 20 x 2

   14 + 40

     54

4) $(13 + 41 - 4) \times 10$

  (54 - 4) x 10

   50 x 10

    500

5) $(8 + 4) \times (10 - 3)$

   12 x 7

    84

6) $(19 + 4) \times 8 - 3$

   23 x 8 - 3

   184 - 3

    181

7) $2 \times 8 + (10 - 6)$

  2 x 8 + 4

   16 + 4

    20

8) $(11 + 5) + 24 \times 4$

   16 + 24 x 4

   16 + 96

    112

9) $(12 + 22 - 2) \times 2$

  (34 - 2) x 2

   32 x 2

    64

10) $(13 + 6) \times (9 - 5)$

   19 x 4

    76

Day 14

1) (19 - 2) x 9 + 3
     17   x 9 + 3
        153   + 3
            156

2) 10 x 4 +(5 + 5)
    10 x 4 + 10
     40   + 10
        50

3) (12 - 3)+ 20 x 4
     9   + 20 x 4
     9   + 80
        89

4) (8 +28 - 6) x 10
   (36 - 6) x 10
     30   x 10
       300

5) (9 + 2) x(10 - 4)
    11   x 6
      66

6) (15 + 6) x 13 - 2
    21   x 13 - 2
      273 - 2
        271

7) 9 x 12 +(3 +10)
   9 x 12 + 13
        + 13
      121

8) (11 + 5)+ 8 x 2
    16 + 8 x 2
    16 + 16
      32

9) (11 +34 - 5) x 4
   (45 - 5) x 4
     40   x 4
      160

10) (14 + 6) x(8 + 4)
    20   x 12
      240

Day 15

1) (14 - 7) x 10 - 4
    7   x 10 - 4
          70   - 4
                66

2)   6 x 10 +(2 + 7)
      6 x 10 +   9
      60   +   9
                 69

3) (12 + 4)+ 16 x 4
      16   + 16 x 4
      16   +   64
                  80

4) (8 +33 - 5) x 12
    (41   - 5) x 12
           36   x 12
                  432

5) (13 + 3) x (14 - 2)
      16   x   12
                 192

6) (19 - 4) x 14 - 4
      15   x 14 - 4
             210   - 4
                   206

7) 10 x 12 +(9 - 10)
     10 x 12 +   -1
            +   -1
                119

8) (11 + 3)+ 12 x 2
      14   + 12 x 2
      14   +   24
                 38

9) (15 +39 - 4) x 2
    (54   - 4) x 2
          50   x 2
                 100

10) (8 + 3) x (13 - 5)
       11   x   8
                   88

Day 16

1) (13 - 3) x 12 - 5
    10   x 12 - 5
       120   - 5
          115

6) (20 - 7) x 9 + 4
    13   x 9 + 4
       117 + 4
          121

2) 6 x 13 + (8 - 4)
  6 x 13 +   4
   78   +   4
      82

7) 9 x 13 + (7 + 9)
  9 x 13 + 16
      + 16
     133

3) (16 + 4) + 14 x 2
   20 + 14 x 2
   20 + 28
      48

8) (16 - 5) + 10 x 2
   11 + 10 x 2
   11 + 20
      31

4) (12 + 17 - 5) x 12
  (29 - 5) x 12
    24   x 12
     288

9) (13 + 17 - 6) x 3
  (30 - 6) x 3
    24   x 3
     72

5) (11 + 6) x (7 - 5)
   17   x 2
     34

10) (12 + 6) x (11 + 2)
   18   x 13
    234

Day 17

1) (18 + 7) x 13 - 5
    25   x 13 - 5
         325   - 5
                  320

2)   6 x 6 +(5 - 2)
      6 x 6 +   3
         36   +   3
                    39

3) (16 - 2)+ 15 x 5
       14   + 15 x 5
       14   +   75
                    89

4) (8 +45 - 5) x 8
    (53   - 5) x 8
           48   x 8
                   384

5) (11 + 6) x(13 - 3)
       17   x   10
                  170

6) (20 - 5) x 12 + 2
       15   x 12 + 2
            180   + 2
                  182

7)   5 x 3 +(7 + 3)
      5 x 3 +   10
         15   +   10
                    25

8) (13 - 2)+ 16 x 8
       11   + 16 x 8
       11   +   128
                  139

9) (8 +30 - 2) x 3
    (38   - 2) x 3
           36   x 3
                  108

10) (15 + 7) x(9 + 2)
        22   x   11
                   242

Day 18

1) (18 - 8) x 13 - 4
        10   x 13 - 4
                130   - 4
                        126

2)   7 x 2 +(8 - 5)
        7 x 2 +   3
        14   +   3
                      17

3) (10 -   5)+ 14 x 2
          5   + 14 x 2
          5   +   28
                        33

4) (13 +25 - 2) x 9
      (38   - 2) x 9
              36   x 9
                      324

5) (15 + 5) x(7 - 5)
          20   x   2
                      40

6) (17 + 3) x 12 - 4
        20   x 12 - 4
                240   - 4
                        236

7)   9 x 12 +(5 - 4)
        9 x 12 +   1
                +   1
                      109

8) (11 -   2)+ 14 x 2
          9   + 14 x 2
          9   +   28
                        37

9) (8 +29 - 5) x 16
      (37   - 5) x 16
              32   x 16
                      512

10) (8 + 7) x(9 + 2)
          15   x   11
                      165

Day 19

1) (11 + 2) x 10 + 2
     13   x 10 + 2
       130 + 2
         132

6) (16 - 8) x 12 + 2
     8   x 12 + 2
      96 + 2
        98

2) 10 x 8 +(9 + 7)
   10 x 8 + 16
    80 + 16
      96

7) 9 x 2 +(2 - 9)
   9 x 2 + -7
    18 + -7
      11

3) (16 + 4)+ 24 x 12
    20 + 24 x 12
    20 + 288
     308

8) (13 - 4)+ 8 x 2
    9 + 8 x 2
    9 + 16
     25

4) (14 + 18 - 4) x 2
  (32 - 4) x 2
    28   x 2
     56

9) (15 + 13 - 4) x 4
  (28 - 4) x 4
    24   x 4
     96

5) (11 + 5) x(12 - 3)
   16   x 9
     144

10) (15 + 6) x(14 + 2)
   21   x 16
     336

Day 20

1) (15 - 6) x 10 - 4

       9   x 10 - 4

         90   - 4

             86

6) (12 + 4) x 10 + 4

      16   x 10 + 4

        160   + 4

            164

2) 10 x 8 +(9 - 10)

   10 x 8 + -1

     80 + -1

         79

7) 4 x 7 +(3 - 4)

   4 x 7 + -1

    28 + -1

       27

3) (9 + 4)+ 16 x 8

   13   + 16 x 8

   13   +   128

        141

8) (11 + 2)+ 16 x 2

   13   + 16 x 2

   13   +   32

       45

4) (12 +40 - 4) x 6

  (52 - 4) x 6

    48   x 6

     288

9) (15 +19 - 6) x 7

  (34 - 6) x 7

    28   x 7

     196

5) (8 + 7) x(14 - 3)

   15   x 11

     165

10) (11 + 7) x(9 - 2)

   18   x 7

    126

Day 21

1) $(8 \times 4 + 4^2) - 2$
$(8 \times 4 + 16) - 2$
$(\quad 32 \quad + 16) - 2$
$48 \quad - 2$
46

2) $5 \times (10 - 5) + 3^2$
$5 \times \quad 5 \quad + 3^2$
$5 \times \quad 5 \quad + 9$
$25 \quad + 9$
34

3) $(14 - 5)^2 + (8 - 4)$
$9^2 \quad + \quad 4$
$81 \quad + \quad 4$
85

4) $(44 - 4^2) - (16 - 2)$
$(44 - 16) - (16 - 2)$
$28 \quad - \quad 14$
14

5) $(30 - 2) - 2 + 7^2$
$28 \quad - 2 + 7^2$
$28 \quad - 2 + 49$
$26 + 49$
75

6) $(57 - 5^2) - (9 - 5)$
$(57 - 25) - (9 - 5)$
$32 \quad - \quad 4$
28

7) $(11 - 5)^2 + (12 - 3)$
$6^2 \quad + \quad 9$
$36 \quad + \quad 9$
45

8) $(32 - 2) - 2 - 3^2$
$30 \quad - 2 - 3^2$
$30 \quad - 2 - 9$
$28 - 9$
19

9) $6 \times (13 - 6) + 7^2$
$6 \times \quad 7 \quad + 7^2$
$6 \times \quad 7 \quad + 49$
$42 \quad + 49$
91

10) $(9 \times 10 - 8^2) + 7$
$(9 \times 10 - 64) + 7$
$(\quad 90 \quad - 64) + 7$
$26 \quad + 7$
33

Day 22

1) $6 \times (9 + 2) - 9^2$
   $6 \times \quad 11 \quad - 9^2$
   $6 \times \quad 11 \quad - 81$
   $\quad 66 \quad\quad - 81$
   $\quad\quad\quad -15$

2) $(54 - 2^2) - (3 + 7)$
   $(54 - 4) - (3 + 7)$
   $\quad 50 \quad - \quad 10$
   $\quad\quad 40$

3) $(55 - 5^2) - (17 - 2)$
   $(55 - 25) - (17 - 2)$
   $\quad 30 \quad - \quad 15$
   $\quad\quad 15$

4) $(6 \times 7 + 3^2) + 10$
   $(6 \times 7 + 9) + 10$
   $(\quad 42 + 9) + 10$
   $\quad\quad 51 \quad\quad + 10$
   $\quad\quad\quad 61$

5) $(34 - 6) - 2 + 4^2$
   $\quad 28 \quad - 2 + 4^2$
   $\quad 28 \quad - 2 + 16$
   $\quad\quad 26 + 16$
   $\quad\quad\quad 42$

6) $(10 - 4)^2 + (8 - 2)$
   $\quad 6^2 \quad + \quad 6$
   $\quad 36 \quad + \quad 6$
   $\quad\quad\quad 42$

7) $(30 - 2) - 14 + 7^2$
   $\quad 28 \quad - 14 + 7^2$
   $\quad 28 \quad - 14 + 49$
   $\quad\quad 14 + 49$
   $\quad\quad\quad 63$

8) $(9 + 2)^2 + (12 - 3)$
   $\quad 11^2 \quad + \quad 9$
   $\quad 121 \quad + \quad 9$
   $\quad\quad\quad 130$

9) $(7 \times 9 - 4^2) + 7$
   $(7 \times 9 - 16) + 7$
   $(\quad 63 - 16) + 7$
   $\quad\quad 47 \quad\quad + 7$
   $\quad\quad\quad 54$

10) $2 \times (8 + 3) - 3^2$
   $2 \times \quad 11 \quad - 3^2$
   $2 \times \quad 11 \quad - 9$
   $\quad 22 \quad\quad\quad 9$
   $\quad\quad\quad 13$

Day 23

1) $(3 + 4)^2 + (12 - 4)$
       7^2 $+$ 8
     49     $+$ 8
                 57

2) $5 \times (10 + 6) + 3^2$
    $5 \times$ 16 $+ 3^2$
    $5 \times$ 16 $+$ 9
     80        $+$ 9
               89

3) $(26 - 2) - 2 + 7^2$
    24    $- 2 + 7^2$
    24    $- 2 + 49$
        $22 + 49$
          71

4) $(64 - 4) - 20 - 5^2$
    60   $- 20 - 5^2$
    60   $- 20 - 25$
        $40 - 25$
         15

5) $(76 - 6^2) - (5 + 5)$
   $(76 - 36) - (5 + 5)$
    40    $-$ 10
         30

6) $5 \times (8 + 5) + 2^2$
   $5 \times$ 13 $+ 2^2$
   $5 \times$ 13 $+$ 4
    65      $+$ 4
         69

7) $(13 \times 8 - 6^2) - 5$
  $(13 \times 8 - 36) - 5$
  $(\quad 104 - 36) - 5$
      68    $- 5$
        63

8) $(7 \times 5 + 8^2) - 10$
  $(7 \times 5 + 64) - 10$
  $(\quad 35 + 64) - 10$
      99   $- 10$
        89

9) $(40 - 2^2) - (12 - 6)$
  $(40 - 4) - (12 - 6)$
    36    $-$ 6
        30

10) $(9 + 3)^2 + (12 - 3)$
   12^2 $+$ 9
   144   $+$ 9
        153

Day 24

1) $(54 - 2^2) - (27 - 2)$
   $(54 - 4) - (27 - 2)$
   $50 \quad - \quad 25$
   $\qquad 25$

2) $(9 + 5)^2 + (10 - 2)$
   $14^2 \quad + \quad 8$
   $196 \quad + \quad 8$
   $\qquad 204$

3) $(9 \times 2 + 4^2) + 4$
   $(9 \times 2 + 16) + 4$
   $(\quad 18 + 16) + 4$
   $\quad 34 \qquad + 4$
   $\qquad 38$

4) $(14 - 4)^2 + (18 - 3)$
   $10^2 \quad + \quad 15$
   $100 \quad + \quad 15$
   $\qquad 115$

5) $6 \times (11 + 5) - 9^2$
   $6 \times \quad 16 \quad - 9^2$
   $6 \times \quad 16 \quad - 81$
   $96 \qquad - 81$
   $\qquad 15$

6) $(50 - 2) - 4 - 4^2$
   $48 \quad - 4 - 4^2$
   $48 \quad - 4 - 16$
   $\qquad 44 - 16$
   $\qquad 28$

7) $(53 - 3) - 2 + 2^2$
   $50 \quad - 2 + 2^2$
   $50 \quad - 2 + 4$
   $\qquad 48 + 4$
   $\qquad 52$

8) $(7 \times 4 - 4^2) - 10$
   $(7 \times 4 - 16) - 10$
   $(\quad 28 - 16) - 10$
   $\qquad 12 \quad - 10$
   $\qquad 2$

9) $(72 - 6^2) - (11 - 2)$
   $(72 - 36) - (11 - 2)$
   $36 \quad - \quad 9$
   $\qquad 27$

10) $4 \times (13 + 6) - 6^2$
   $4 \times \quad 19 \quad - 6^2$
   $4 \times \quad 19 \quad - 36$
   $76 \qquad 36$
   $\qquad 40$

Day 25

1) $(13 \times 10 - 9^2) - 8$
$(13 \times 10 - 81) - 8$
$(130 - 81) - 8$
$49 - 8$
41

2) $(8 - 2)^2 + (18 - 6)$
$6^2 + 12$
$36 + 12$
48

3) $(55 - 5) - 2 - 4^2$
$50 - 2 - 4^2$
$50 - 2 - 16$
$48 - 16$
32

4) $(72 - 6^2) - (-2 + 4)$
$(72 - 36) - (-2 + 4)$
$36 - 2$
34

5) $(55 - 5) - 2 + 2^2$
$50 - 2 + 2^2$
$50 - 2 + 4$
$48 + 4$
52

6) $(44 - 4^2) - (-2 + 4)$
$(44 - 16) - (-2 + 4)$
$28 - 2$
26

7) $(10 \times 7 + 2^2) - 3$
$(10 \times 7 + 4) - 3$
$(70 + 4) - 3$
$74 - 3$
71

8) $3 \times (10 + 3) - 5^2$
$3 \times 13 - 5^2$
$3 \times 13 - 25$
$39 - 25$
14

9) $(6 + 3)^2 + (15 - 5)$
$9^2 + 10$
$81 + 10$
91

10) $3 \times (9 - 4) - 3^2$
$3 \times 5 - 3^2$
$3 \times 5 - 9$
$15 - 9$
6

Day 26

1) $(28 - 2^2) - (6 - 2)$
   $(28 - 4) - (6 - 2)$
   $24 \quad - \quad 4$
   $\quad\quad\quad 20$

2) $4 \times (12 + 4) - 6^2$
   $4 \times \quad 16 \quad - 6^2$
   $4 \times \quad 16 \quad - 36$
   $64 \quad\quad\quad - 36$
   $\quad\quad\quad 28$

3) $(3 \times 7 - 2^2) + 8$
   $(3 \times 7 - 4) + 8$
   $(\quad 21 \; - \; 4) + 8$
   $\quad 17 \quad + 8$
   $\quad\quad\quad 25$

4) $(41 - 5) - 3 - 3^2$
   $36 \quad - 3 - 3^2$
   $36 \quad - 3 - 9$
   $\quad\quad 33 - 9$
   $\quad\quad\quad 24$

5) $8 \times (10 - 6) + 3^2$
   $8 \times \quad 4 \quad + 3^2$
   $8 \times \quad 4 \quad + 9$
   $32 \quad\quad + 9$
   $\quad\quad 41$

6) $(3 \times 10 - 6^2) + 7$
   $(3 \times 10 - 36) + 7$
   $(\quad 30 \; - 36) + 7$
   $\quad -6 \quad + 7$
   $\quad\quad\quad 1$

7) $(61 - 5^2) - (-2 + 5)$
   $(61 - 25) - (-2 + 5)$
   $36 \quad - \quad 3$
   $\quad\quad\quad 33$

8) $(12 - 4)^2 + (12 - 6)$
   $8^2 \quad + \quad 6$
   $64 \quad + \quad 6$
   $\quad\quad\quad 70$

9) $(8 - 2)^2 + (14 - 2)$
   $6^2 \quad + \quad 12$
   $36 \quad + \quad 12$
   $\quad\quad\quad 48$

10) $(65 - 5) - 20 + 3^2$
   $60 \quad - 20 + 3^2$
   $60 \quad - 20 + 9$
   $\quad\quad 40 + 9$
   $\quad\quad 49$

Day 27

1) $(34 - 4) - 15 + 5^2$
    30    $- 15 + 5^2$
    30    $- 15 + 25$
          $15 + 25$
           40

2) $8 \times (9 - 5) + 8^2$
    $8 \times$ 4 $+ 8^2$
    $8 \times$ 4 $+ 64$
    32        $+ 64$
          96

3) $(34 - 2) - 8 + 4^2$
    32    $- 8 + 4^2$
    32    $- 8 + 16$
        $24 + 16$
         40

4) $(55 - 5^2) - (13 - 3)$
    $(55 - 25) - (13 - 3)$
    30    $-$ 10
         20

5) $(9 + 2)^2 + (14 - 7)$
    11^2 $+$ 7
    121    $+$ 7
        128

6) $(9 \times 8 - 3^2) + 2$
    $(9 \times 8 - 9) + 2$
    $(72 - 9) + 2$
    63    $+ 2$
        65

7) $(34 - 2^2) - (8 - 5)$
    $(34 - 4) - (8 - 5)$
    30    $-$ 3
        27

8) $7 \times (10 + 2) + 4^2$
    $7 \times$ 12 $+ 4^2$
    $7 \times$ 12 $+ 16$
    84        $+ 16$
        100

9) $(10 \times 4 - 3^2) + 5$
    $(10 \times 4 - 9) + 5$
    $(40 - 9) + 5$
    31    $+ 5$
        36

10) $(7 + 2)^2 + (20 - 5)$
    9^2 $+$ 15
    81    $+$ 15
        96

Day 28

1) $(34 - 4) - 15 + 5^2$

    30     $- 15 + 5^2$

    30     $- 15 + 25$

             15 + 25

                40

2) $8 \times (9 - 5) + 8^2$

    $8 \times$ 4 $+ 8^2$

    $8 \times$ 4 $+ 64$

    32          $+ 64$

                96

3) $(34 - 2) - 8 + 4^2$

    32     $- 8 + 4^2$

    32     $- 8 + 16$

           24 + 16

                40

4) $(55 - 5^2) - (13 - 3)$

   $(55 - 25) - (13 - 3)$

    30       $-$ 10

                20

5) $(9 + 2)^2 + (14 - 7)$

    11^2 +   7

    121   +   7

             128

6) $(9 \times 8 - 3^2) + 2$

   $(9 \times 8 - 9) + 2$

   $(\quad 72 - 9) + 2$

        63   + 2

             65

7) $(34 - 2^2) - (8 - 5)$

   $(34 - 4) - (8 - 5)$

    30      $-$ 3

             27

8) $7 \times (10 + 2) + 4^2$

    $7 \times$ 12 $+ 4^2$

    $7 \times$ 12 $+ 16$

    84        $+ 16$

           100

9) $(10 \times 4 - 3^2) + 5$

   $(10 \times 4 - 9) + 5$

   $(\quad 40 - 9) + 5$

        31   + 5

            36

10) $(7 + 2)^2 + (20 - 5)$

    9^2 +   15

    81   +   15

           96

Day 29

1) $(5 \times 6 - 2^2) + 8$
   $(5 \times 6 - 4) + 8$
   $(\quad 30 - 4) + 8$
          $26 \quad + 8$
               34

2) $(42 - 2) - 10 - 4^2$
      $40 \quad - 10 - 4^2$
      $40 \quad - 10 - 16$
          $30 - 16$
             14

3) $(9 + 3)^2 + (15 - 3)$
     $12^2 \quad + \quad 12$
   $144 \quad + \quad 12$
             156

4) $(36 - 4) - 2 - 2^2$
     $32 \quad - 2 - 2^2$
     $32 \quad - 2 - 4$
         $30 - 4$
           26

5) $(7 \times 7 + 3^2) + 6$
   $(7 \times 7 + 9) + 6$
   $(\quad 49 + 9) + 6$
         $58 \quad + 6$
           61

6) $(9 + 5)^2 + (18 - 6)$
     $14^2 \quad + \quad 12$
    $196 \quad + \quad 12$
           208

7) $(52 - 4^2) - (1 + 2)$
   $(52 - 16) - (1 + 2)$
    $36 \quad - \quad 3$
          33

8) $(96 - 6^2) - (19 - 4)$
   $(96 - 36) - (19 - 4)$
    $60 \quad - \quad 15$
          45

9) $2 \times (12 - 5) - 5^2$
   $2 \times \quad 7 \quad - 5^2$
   $2 \times \quad 7 \quad - 25$
     $14 \quad\quad - 25$
          -11

10) $8 \times (11 + 3) + 3^2$
   $8 \times \quad 14 \quad + 3^2$
   $8 \times \quad 14 \quad + 9$
   $112 \quad\quad + 9$
          121

Day 30

1) $(35 - 5) - 10 - 4^2$
   $30 \quad - 10 - 4^2$
   $30 \quad - 10 - 16$
   $\qquad 20 - 16$
   $\qquad\qquad 4$

2) $(64 - 4) - 6 - 2^2$
   $60 \quad - 6 - 2^2$
   $60 \quad - 6 - 4$
   $\qquad 54 - 4$
   $\qquad\qquad 50$

3) $(7 \times 3 + 5^2) + 8$
   $(7 \times 3 + 25) + 8$
   $(\quad 21 \quad + 25) + 8$
   $\qquad 46 \qquad + 8$
   $\qquad\qquad 54$

4) $3 \times (9 + 2) - 4^2$
   $3 \times \quad 11 \quad - 4^2$
   $3 \times \quad 11 \quad - 16$
   $\quad 33 \qquad\quad - 16$
   $\qquad\qquad 17$

5) $(36 - 2^2) - (2 + 2)$
   $(36 - 4) - (2 + 2)$
   $\quad 32 \qquad - \quad 4$
   $\qquad\qquad 28$

6) $(8 - 4)^2 + (18 - 2)$
   $\quad 4^2 \qquad + \qquad 16$
   $\quad 16 \qquad + \qquad 16$
   $\qquad\qquad 32$

7) $2 \times (11 + 5) + 6^2$
   $2 \times \quad 16 \quad + 6^2$
   $2 \times \quad 16 \quad + 36$
   $\quad 32 \qquad\quad + 36$
   $\qquad\qquad 68$

8) $(7 \times 6 + 7^2) + 4$
   $(7 \times 6 + 49) + 4$
   $(\quad 42 \quad + 49) + 4$
   $\qquad 91 \qquad + 4$
   $\qquad\qquad 95$

9) $(45 - 3^2) - (5 - 2)$
   $(45 - 9) - (5 - 2)$
   $\quad 36 \qquad - \qquad 3$
   $\qquad\qquad 33$

10) $(10 + 2)^2 + (20 - 4)$
   $\quad 12^2 \qquad + \qquad 16$
   $\quad 144 \qquad + \qquad 16$
   $\qquad\qquad 160$

Day 31

1) ((10 + 3) x 5) - 4
   (13   x 5) - 4
        65   - 4
              61

2) (9 + (14 - 7)) x 5
  (9 +   7   ) x 5
      16   x 5
          80

3) (12 + (14 - 2)) x 4
  (12 +   12   ) x 4
      24   x 4
          96

4) ((18 - 3) + 7) + 13
  (15   + 7) + 13
       22   + 13
          35

5) 15 + ((18 + 6) + 6)
  15 + (24   + 6)
  15 +   30
          45

6) (6 + (14 - 7 + 9))
  (6 + (7   + 9))
  (6 +   16   )
        22

7) 19 + (3 x (11 - 4))
  19 + (3 x   7   )
  19 +   21
       40

8) (12 + (16 - 8 + 4))
  (12 + (8   + 4))
  (12 +   12   )
       24

9) 14 + ((16 - 3) + 2)
  14 + (13   + 2)
  14 +   15
      29

10) 6 + (3 + (13 + 7))
  6 + (3 +   20   )
  6 +   23
     29

Day 32

1) 8 + ((9 - 3) x 6)
    8 + (6   x 6)
    8 +   36
            44

2) ((13 - 6) x 2) + 12
   (7   x 2) + 12
        14   + 12
           26

3) (16 + (8 - 2)) x 4
   (16 +   6   ) x 4
        22   x 4
           88

4) 12 + (2 x (14 + 3))
   12 + (2 x   17   )
   12 +   34
        46

5) 8 + (6 x (10 + 6))
   8 + (6 x   16   )
   8 +   96
     104

6) 15 + ((10 + 3) x 4)
   15 + (13   x 4)
   15 +   52
        67

7) (11 + (8 - 2)) + 5
   (11 +   6   ) + 5
       17   + 5
         22

8) (4 + (20 - 4 + 8))
   (4 + (16   + 8))
   (4 +   24   )
       28

9) (8 + (20 - 4 - 7))
   (8 + (16   - 7))
   (8 +   9   )
      17

10) ((10 - 7) + 4) + 12
   (3   + 4) + 12
       7   + 12
       19

Day 33

1) 12 + (8 x (12 + 8))
   12 + (8 x   20)
   12 +   160
     172

2) ((15 + 2) + 4) + 3
   (17   + 4) + 3
    21   + 3
      24

3) 15 + ((15 - 4) + 6)
   15 + (11   + 6)
   15 +   17
      32

4) 2 + (4 + (11 + 2))
   2 + (4 +   13)
   2 +   17
     19

5) 19 + ((16 + 7) + 6)
   19 + (23   + 6)
   19 +   29
     48

6) (13 + (18 - 2 + 2))
   (13 + (16   + 2))
   (13 +   18   )
     31

7) (18 + (8 - 2)) + 3
   (18 +   6   ) + 3
     24   + 3
      27

8) ((12 - 8) x 5) - 12
   (4   x 5) - 12
     20   - 12
       8

9) (16 + (12 - 6)) + 2
   (16 +   6   ) + 2
     22   + 2
      24

10) (9 + (15 - 3 - 3))
   (9 + (12   - 3))
   (9 +   9   )
     18

Day 34

1) 9 + ((11 + 6) + 5)
    9 + (17   + 5)
    9 +   22
              31

2) (9 + (15 - 5)) x 5
   (9 +   10) x 5
        19   x 5
             95

3) (10 + (14 - 7 - 8))
   (10 + (7   - 8))
   (10 +   -1   )
          9

4) (15 + (20 - 2)) x 6
   (15 +   18) x 6
        33   x 6
           198

5) 5 + (5 x (10 - 2))
    5 + (5 x   8)
    5 +   40
       45

6) ((13 - 5) x 4) + 11
   (8   x 4) + 11
        32   + 11
          43

7) (7 + (18 - 2 + 5))
   (7 + (16   + 5))
   (7 +   21   )
        28

8) 7 + ((17 + 2) x 2)
    7 + (19   x 2)
    7 +   38
        45

9) ((13 + 6) x 2) + 5
   (19   x 2) + 5
       38   + 5
         43

10) 3 + (9 x (9 + 5))
    3 + (9 x 14)
    3 + 126
      129

Day 35

1) ((18 - 2) + 2) - 6
   (16   + 2) - 6
         18   - 6
             12

2) (6 +(12 - 6 + 9))
   (6 +(6   + 9))
   (6 +   15   )
         21

3) 18 +(7 x (10 - 3))
   18 +(7 x   7   )
   18 +   49
       67

4) ((11 +4) + 6) - 5
   (15   + 6) - 5
       21   - 5
         16

5) (7 +(15 - 3 + 2))
   (7 +(12   + 2))
   (7 +   14   )
       21

6) (11 +(12 - 2)) + 4
   (11 +   10   ) + 4
       21   + 4
         25

7) 2 +(3 x (16 - 3))
   2 +(3 x   13   )
   2 +   39
       41

8) (17 +(12 - 3)) x 7
   (17 +   9   ) x 7
       26   x 7
        182

9) 8 +((11 - 2) x 5)
   8 +(9   x 5)
   8 +   45
        53

10) 7 +((18 - 6) + 6)
   7 +(12   + 6)
   7 +   18
        25

Day 36

1) (9 +(14 - 7 - 6))
   (9 +(7 - 6))
   (9 +   1   )
       10

2) 3 +(7 +(10 + 6))
   3 +(7 + 16)
   3 +   23
      26

3) (15 +(18 - 2)) + 2
   (15 + 16) + 2
     31   + 2
        33

4) ((14 - 4) + 6) + 6
   (10 + 6) + 6
     16   + 6
        22

5) 11 + ((18 - 4) x 5)
   11 + (14   x 5)
   11 +   70
       81

6) ((16 - 2) x 2) + 9
   (14 x 2) + 9
     28   + 9
       37

7) 8 + ((17 + 3) x 4)
   8 + (20   x 4)
   8 +   80
      88

8) 2 +(5 + (16 + 8))
   2 +(5 + 24)
   2 +   29
      31

9) (13 +(18 - 6 + 7))
   (13 +(12 + 7))
   (13 +   19   )
       32

10) (16 +(10 - 5)) + 4
   (16 + 5   ) + 4
     21   + 4
       25

Day 37

1) 9 + (4 x (14 + 2))
     9 + (4 x   16   )
     9 +   64
              73

2) ((18 - 6) x 3) + 3
     (12   x 3) + 3
             36   + 3
                   39

3) 9 + ((12 - 5) x 3)
     9 + (7   x 3)
     9 +   21
                   30

4) (2 + (14 - 2 + 3))
     (2 + (12   + 3))
     (2 +   15   )
                 17

5) (2 + (12 - 4 - 3))
     (2 + (8   - 3))
     (2 +   5   )
                7

6) (18 + (8 - 4)) + 5
     (18 +   4   ) + 5
              22   + 5
                    27

7) ((15 + 8) x 6) - 3
     (23   x 6) - 3
            138   - 3
                  135

8) 6 + (9 + (12 - 7))
     6 + (9 +   5   )
     6 +   14
                20

9) 13 + ((14 - 3) x 2)
     13 + (11   x 2)
     13 +   22
                   35

10) (17 + (12 - 3)) x 2
      (17 +   9   ) x 2
               26   x 2
                     52

Day 38

1) 15 + (2 + (13 - 2))
     15 + (2 +   11)
     15 +   13
               28

2) (5 + (14 - 2 - 7))
    (5 + (12 - 7))
    (5 +   5   )
               10

3) ((17 + 3) x 7) - 8
    (20 x 7) - 8
          140   - 8
                132

4) (11 + (12 - 3)) x 4
    (11 +   9   ) x 4
          20   x 4
                80

5) ((14 + 5) x 2) + 10
    (19 x 2) + 10
          38   + 10
                48

6) 19 + ((15 - 3) + 6)
     19 + (12   + 6)
     19 +   18
                    37

7) (17 + (14 - 2)) + 6
    (17 +   12) + 6
           29   + 6
                 35

8) 16 + ((17 + 6) + 4)
     16 + (23   + 4)
     16 +   27
                   43

9) (7 + (8 - 4 + 4))
    (7 + (4   + 4))
    (7 +   8   )
                15

10) 18 + (9 x (9 - 5))
      18 + (9 x   4)
      18 +   36
              54

Day 39

1) 8 + ((12 - 3) + 4)
     8 + (9   + 4)
     8 +   13
                 21

2) 15 + (4 + (14 + 5))
     15 + (4 +   19   )
     15 +   23
                 38

3) ((9 - 6) x 5) - 6
     (3   x 5) - 6
            15   - 6
                   9

4) (10 + (15 - 3 + 2))
     (10 + (12   + 2))
     (10 +   14   )
                 24

5) (17 + (10 - 5)) x 4
     (17 +   5   ) x 4
            22   x 4
                    88

6) 7 + (3 x (17 - 6))
     7 + (3 x   11   )
     7 +   33
                40

7) ((12 + 5) + 3) + 11
     (17   + 3) + 11
             20   + 11
                    31

8) (9 + (16 - 4 - 2))
     (9 + (12   - 2))
     (9 +   10   )
                   19

9) 9 + ((14 - 7) + 4)
     9 + (7   + 4)
     9 +   11
                 20

10) (15 + (12 - 6)) + 5
     (15 +   6   ) + 5
            21   + 5
                    26

Day 40

1) (4 +(18 - 3 - 6))
    (4 +(15   - 6))
    (4 +   9   )
        13

2) ((9 +7) + 3) + 9
    (16   + 3) + 9
        19   + 9
           28

3) ((12 +5) x 7) + 5
    (17   x 7) + 5
      119   + 5
         124

4) (16 +(16 - 2)) + 3
    (16 +   14   ) + 3
        30   + 3
          33

5)   7 + ((15 + 3) x 6)
    7 + (18   x 6)
    7 +
        115

6) (15 +(15 - 3)) x 5
    (15 +   12   ) x 5
        27   x 5
          135

7)   5 +(8 x (15 + 5))
    5 +(8 x   20   )
    5 +   160
      165

8)   18 + ((10 - 7) x 2)
    18 +(3   x 2)
    18 +   6
      24

9)   16 +(6 + (12 - 3))
    16 +(6 +   9   )
    16 +   15
      31

10) (11 +(15 - 5 + 7))
    (11 +(10   + 7))
    (11 +   17   )
      28

Day 41

1) $((4+2)^2 \times 6) - 2^2$
$(\quad 6^2 \quad \times 6) - 2^2$
$(\quad 36 \quad \times 6) - 2^2$
$\qquad 216 \qquad - 2^2$
$\qquad 216 \qquad - 4$
$\qquad\qquad 212$

2) $((12-3)+(8-4)^2)$
$(\quad 9 \quad +(\quad 4 \quad)^2)$
$(\quad 9 \quad + \quad 16 \quad)$
$\qquad 25$

3) $((11+7)+(18-3)^2)$
$(\quad 18 \quad +(\quad 15 \quad)^2)$
$(\quad 18 \quad + \quad 225 \quad)$
$\qquad 243$

4) $10+((9-3) \times 4^2)$
$10+(\quad 6 \quad \times 4^2)$
$10+(\quad 6 \quad \times 16)$
$10+\qquad 96$
$\qquad 106$

5) $(3^2+(14-7+3^2))$
$(3^2+(14-7+9))$
$(3^2+(\quad 7 \quad +9))$
$(3^2+\qquad 16 \qquad)$
$(9+\qquad 16 \qquad)$
$\qquad 25$

6) $((9-2)^2+5)+5^2$
$(\quad 7^2 \quad +5)+5^2$
$(\quad 49 \quad +5)+5^2$
$\qquad 54 \qquad +5^2$
$\qquad 54 \qquad +25$
$\qquad\qquad 79$

7) $(3^2+(14-7+4^2))$
$(3^2+(14-7+16))$
$(3^2+(\quad 7 \quad +16))$
$(3^2+\qquad 23 \qquad)$
$(9+\qquad 23 \qquad)$
$\qquad 32$

8) $5+(3+(11-2)^2)$
$5+(3+\quad 9^2 \quad)$
$5+(3+\quad 81 \quad)$
$5+\qquad 84$
$\qquad 89$

9) $12+(2+(11-6)^2)$
$12+(2+\quad 5^2 \quad)$
$12+(2+\quad 25 \quad)$
$12+\qquad 27$
$\qquad 39$

10) $16+((11-5)+3^2)$
$16+(\quad 6 \quad +3^2)$
$16+(\quad 6 \quad +9)$
$16+\qquad 15$
$\qquad 31$

Day 42

1) $14 + ((12 + 4) \times 3^2)$
$14 + (\quad 16 \quad \times 3^2)$
$14 + (\quad 16 \quad \times 9)$
$14 + \quad\quad\quad 144$
$\quad\quad\quad\quad 158$

2) $5 + (6 \times (6 + 3)^2)$
$5 + (6 \times \quad 9^2 \quad)$
$5 + (6 \times \quad 81 \quad)$
$5 + \quad 486$
$\quad\quad\quad 491$

3) $14 + ((9 + 2) + 6^2)$
$14 + (\quad 11 \quad + 6^2)$
$14 + (\quad 11 \quad + 36)$
$14 + \quad\quad\quad 47$
$\quad\quad\quad\quad 61$

4) $((11 - 2)^2 \times 7) - 2^2$
$(\quad 9^2 \quad \times 7) - 2^2$
$(\quad 81 \quad \times 7) - 2^2$
$\quad\quad 567 \quad\quad - 2^2$
$\quad\quad 567 \quad\quad - 4$
$\quad\quad\quad\quad 563$

5) $(6^2 + (24 - 2 + 4^2))$
$(6^2 + (24 - 2 + 16))$
$(6^2 + (22 \quad + 16))$
$(6^2 + \quad\quad 38 \quad\quad)$
$(36 + \quad\quad 38 \quad\quad)$
$\quad\quad 74$

6) $((11 - 7) + (15 - 5)^2)$
$(\quad 4 \quad + (10 \quad)^2)$
$(\quad 4 \quad + \quad 100 \quad)$
$\quad\quad\quad 104$

7) $(7^2 + (20 - 2 + 2^2))$
$(7^2 + (20 - 2 + 4))$
$(7^2 + (18 \quad + 4))$
$(7^2 + \quad\quad 22 \quad\quad)$
$(49 + \quad\quad 22 \quad\quad)$
$\quad\quad\quad 71$

8) $((14 + 5) + (10 - 5)^2)$
$(\quad 19 \quad + (5 \quad)^2)$
$(\quad 19 \quad + \quad 25 \quad)$
$\quad\quad\quad 44$

9) $((10 - 5)^2 \times 3) - 2^2$
$(\quad 5^2 \quad \times 3) - 2^2$
$(\quad 25 \quad \times 3) - 2^2$
$\quad\quad\quad 75 \quad\quad - 2^2$
$\quad\quad\quad 75 \quad\quad - 4$
$\quad\quad\quad\quad 71$

10) $9 + (8 \times (3 + 2)^2)$
$9 + (8 \times \quad 5^2 \quad)$
$9 + (8 \times \quad 25 \quad)$
$9 + \quad 200$
$\quad\quad 208$

Day 43

1) $17 + (9 + (10 - 3)^2)$
  $17 + (9 + \quad 7^2 \quad)$
  $17 + (9 + \quad 49 \quad)$
  $17 + \quad 58$
  $\qquad 75$

2) $((10 - 4) + (12 - 2)^2)$
  $(\quad 6 \quad + (\quad 10 \quad)^2)$
  $(\quad 6 \quad + \quad 100 \quad)$
  $\qquad 106$

3) $((6 + 4)^2 + 2) + 4^2$
  $(\quad 10^2 \quad + 2) + 4^2$
  $(\quad 100 \quad + 2) + 4^2$
  $\qquad 102 \quad + 4^2$
  $\qquad 102 \quad + 16$
  $\qquad 118$

4) $(7^2 + (12 - 6 + 2^2))$
  $(7^2 + (12 - 6 + 4))$
  $(7^2 + (6 \quad + 4))$
  $(7^2 + \quad 10 \quad)$
  $(49 + \quad 10 \quad)$
  $\qquad 59$

5) $14 + ((18 - 2) \times 4^2)$
  $14 + (\quad 16 \quad \times 4^2)$
  $14 + (\quad 16 \quad \times 16)$
  $14 + \quad 256$
  $\qquad 270$

6) $8 + ((13 + 7) + 5^2)$
  $8 + (\quad 20 \quad + 5^2)$
  $8 + (\quad 20 \quad + 25)$
  $8 + \quad 45$
  $\qquad 53$

7) $((11 - 3)^2 \times 2) + 6^2$
  $(\quad 8^2 \quad \times 2) + 6^2$
  $(\quad 64 \quad \times 2) + 6^2$
  $\qquad 128 \quad + 6^2$
  $\qquad 128 \quad + 36$
  $\qquad 164$

8) $5 + (10 \times (9 - 5)^2)$
  $5 + (10 \times \quad 4^2 \quad)$
  $5 + (10 \times \quad 16 \quad)$
  $5 + \quad 160$
  $\qquad 165$

9) $(5^2 + (24 - 2 + 4^2))$
  $(5^2 + (24 - 2 + 16))$
  $(5^2 + (22 \quad + 16))$
  $(5^2 + \quad 38 \quad)$
  $(25 + \quad 38 \quad)$
  $\qquad 63$

10) $((12 + 4) + (12 - 6)^2)$
  $(\quad 16 \quad + (\quad 6 \quad)^2)$
  $(\quad 16 \quad + \quad 36 \quad)$
  $\qquad 52$

Day 44

1) $((11 - 5)^2 \times 7) + 6^2$
$(\quad 6^2 \quad \times 7) + 6^2$
$(\quad 36 \quad \times 7) + 6^2$
$\qquad 252 \qquad + 6^2$
$\qquad 252 \qquad + 36$
$\qquad\qquad 288$

2) $18 + ((13 - 3) + 4^2)$
$18 + (\qquad 10 \quad + 4^2)$
$18 + (\qquad 10 \quad + 16)$
$18 + \qquad\qquad 26$
$\qquad\qquad 44$

3) $13 + (8 \times (9 - 5)^2)$
$13 + (8 \times \quad 4^2 \quad)$
$13 + (8 \times \quad 16 \quad)$
$13 + \quad 128$
$\qquad 141$

4) $(6^2 + (24 - 12 + 4^2))$
$(6^2 + (24 - 12 + 16))$
$(6^2 + (\quad 12 \quad + 16))$
$(6^2 + \qquad 28 \qquad)$
$(36 + \qquad 28 \qquad)$
$\qquad 64$

5) $(3^2 + (8 - 4 + 3^2))$
$(3^2 + (8 - 4 + 9))$
$(3^2 + (\quad 4 \quad + 9))$
$(3^2 + \qquad 13 \qquad)$
$(9 + \qquad 13 \qquad)$
$\qquad 22$

6) $((10 - 2) + (18 - 6)^2)$
$(\qquad 8 \quad + (\quad 12 \quad)^2)$
$(\qquad 8 \quad + \quad 144 \quad)$
$\qquad 152$

7) $14 + (4 \times (10 - 4)^2)$
$14 + (4 \times \quad 6^2 \quad)$
$14 + (4 \times \quad 36 \quad)$
$14 + \quad 144$
$\qquad 158$

8) $((11 - 3)^2 + 5) + 4^2$
$(\quad 8^2 \quad + 5) + 4^2$
$(\quad 64 \quad + 5) + 4^2$
$\qquad\qquad 69 \qquad + 4^2$
$\qquad\qquad 69 \qquad + 16$
$\qquad\qquad 85$

9) $16 + ((9 + 6) \times 5^2)$
$16 + (\quad 15 \quad \times 5^2)$
$16 + (\quad 15 \quad \times 25)$
$16 + \qquad 375$
$\qquad 391$

10) $((12 - 4) + (24 - 3)^2)$
$(\qquad 8 \quad + (\quad 21 \quad)^2)$
$(\qquad 8 \quad + \quad 441 \quad)$
$\qquad 449$

Day 45

1) $12 + (5 \times (5 + 3)^2)$
$12 + (5 \times \quad 8^2 \quad)$
$12 + (5 \times \quad 64 \quad)$
$12 + \quad 320$
$\qquad 332$

2) $(3^2 + (18 - 2 + 4^2))$
$(3^2 + (18 - 2 + 16))$
$(3^2 + (\quad 16 \quad + 16))$
$(3^2 + \quad 32 \quad)$
$(9 + \quad 32 \quad)$
$\qquad 41$

3) $((11 - 2)^2 + 6) + 6^2$
$(\quad 9^2 \quad + 6) + 6^2$
$(\quad 81 \quad + 6) + 6^2$
$\qquad 87 \qquad + 6^2$
$\qquad 87 \qquad + 36$
$\qquad 123$

4) $((11 - 7) + (15 - 3)^2)$
$(\quad 4 \quad + (\quad 12 \quad)^2)$
$(\quad 4 \quad + \quad 144 \quad)$
$\qquad 148$

5) $24 + ((15 + 4) \times 2^2)$
$24 + (\quad 19 \quad \times 2^2)$
$24 + (\quad 19 \quad \times 4)$
$24 + \qquad 76$
$\qquad 100$

6) $((12 - 7) + (15 - 5)^2)$
$(\quad 5 \quad + (\quad 10 \quad)^2)$
$(\quad 5 \quad + \quad 100 \quad)$
$\qquad 105$

7) $2 + (8 \times (11 - 5)^2)$
$2 + (8 \times \quad 6^2 \quad)$
$2 + (8 \times \quad 36 \quad)$
$2 + \quad 288$
$\qquad 290$

8) $8 + ((12 + 2) \times 6^2)$
$8 + (\quad 14 \quad \times 6^2)$
$8 + (\quad 14 \quad \times 36)$
$8 + \qquad 504$
$\qquad 512$

9) $(3^2 + (15 - 3 + 2^2))$
$(3^2 + (15 - 3 + 4))$
$(3^2 + (\quad 12 \quad + 4))$
$(3^2 + \qquad 16 \qquad)$
$(9 + \qquad 16 \qquad)$
$\qquad 25$

10) $((9 - 2)^2 \times 4) + 8^2$
$(\quad 7^2 \quad \times 4) + 8^2$
$(\quad 49 \quad \times 4) + 8^2$
$\qquad 196 \qquad + 8^2$
$\qquad 196 \qquad + 64$
$\qquad 260$

Day 46

1) $12 + ((18 + 7) + 6^2)$
    $12 + (\quad 25 \quad + 6^2)$
    $12 + (\quad 25 \quad + 36)$
    $12 + \quad\quad 61$
    $\quad\quad\quad 73$

2) $4 + (6 + (6 + 5)^2)$
    $4 + (6 + \quad 11^2 \quad)$
    $4 + (6 + \quad 121 \quad)$
    $4 + \quad 127$
    $\quad\quad 131$

3) $(3^2 + (15 - 3 + 4^2))$
    $(3^2 + (15 - 3 + 16))$
    $(3^2 + (12 \quad + 16))$
    $(3^2 + \quad 28 \quad)$
    $(9 + \quad 28 \quad)$
    $\quad 37$

4) $((3 + 2)^2 + 3) - 3^2$
    $(\quad 5^2 \quad + 3) - 3^2$
    $(\quad 25 \quad + 3) - 3^2$
    $\quad 28 \quad - 3^2$
    $\quad 28 \quad - 9$
    $\quad\quad 19$

5) $((16 + 7) + (8 - 2)^2)$
    $(\quad 23 \quad + (6 \quad)^2)$
    $(\quad 23 \quad + \quad 36 \quad)$
    $\quad 59$

6) $((18 + 3) + (14 - 7)^2)$
    $(\quad 21 \quad + (7 \quad)^2)$
    $(\quad 21 \quad + \quad 49 \quad)$
    $\quad\quad 70$

7) $14 + (5 + (6 + 4)^2)$
    $14 + (5 + \quad 10^2 \quad)$
    $14 + (5 + \quad 100 \quad)$
    $14 + \quad 105$
    $\quad\quad 119$

8) $14 + ((12 - 2) + 5^2)$
    $14 + (\quad 10 \quad + 5^2)$
    $14 + (\quad 10 \quad + 25)$
    $14 + \quad\quad 35$
    $\quad\quad\quad 49$

9) $(7^2 + (14 - 2 + 5^2))$
    $(7^2 + (14 - 2 + 25))$
    $(7^2 + (12 \quad + 25))$
    $(7^2 + \quad 37 \quad)$
    $(49 + \quad 37 \quad)$
    $\quad 86$

10) $((10 - 5)^2 \times 7) + 3^2$
    $(\quad 5^2 \quad \times 7) + 3^2$
    $(\quad 25 \quad \times 7) + 3^2$
    $\quad\quad 175 \quad + 3^2$
    $\quad\quad 175 \quad + 9$
    $\quad\quad 184$

Day 47

1) $((9 - 6)^2 \times 2) + 6^2$
$(\quad 3^2 \quad \times 2) + 6^2$
$(\quad 9 \quad \times 2) + 6^2$
$\qquad 18 \qquad + 6^2$
$\qquad 18 \qquad + 36$
$\qquad\qquad 54$

2) $18 + ((15 + 4) \times 3^2)$
$18 + (\quad 19 \quad \times 3^2)$
$18 + (\quad 19 \quad \times 9)$
$18 + \qquad 171$
$\qquad\qquad 189$

3) $13 + (8 + (11 - 5)^2)$
$13 + (8 + \quad 6^2 \quad)$
$13 + (8 + \quad 36 \quad)$
$13 + \qquad 44$
$\qquad\qquad 57$

4) $((11 + 3) + (15 - 5)^2)$
$(\quad 14 \quad + (\quad 10 \quad)^2)$
$(\quad 14 \quad + \quad 100 \quad)$
$\qquad\qquad 114$

5) $6 + (9 + (5 + 5)^2)$
$6 + (9 + \quad 10^2 \quad)$
$6 + (9 + \quad 100 \quad)$
$6 + \qquad 109$
$\qquad\qquad 115$

6) $((3 + 2)^2 + 5) + 8^2$
$(\quad 5^2 \quad + 5) + 8^2$
$(\quad 25 \quad + 5) + 8^2$
$\qquad 30 \qquad + 8^2$
$\qquad 30 \qquad + 64$
$\qquad\qquad 94$

7) $8 + ((11 - 6) \times 4^2)$
$8 + (\quad 5 \quad \times 4^2)$
$8 + (\quad 5 \quad \times 16)$
$8 + \qquad 80$
$\qquad\qquad 88$

8) $(6^2 + (24 - 12 + 3^2))$
$(6^2 + (24 - 12 + 9))$
$(6^2 + (\quad 12 \quad + 9))$
$(6^2 + \qquad 21 \qquad)$
$(36 + \qquad 21 \qquad)$
$\qquad\qquad 57$

9) $(3^2 + (8 - 4 + 2^2))$
$(3^2 + (8 - 4 + 4))$
$(3^2 + (\quad 4 \quad + 4))$
$(3^2 + \qquad 8 \qquad)$
$(9 + \qquad 8 \qquad)$
$\qquad\qquad 17$

10) $((14 - 6) + (12 - 6)^2)$
$(\quad 8 \quad + (\quad 6 \quad)^2)$
$(\quad 8 \quad + \quad 36 \quad)$
$\qquad\qquad 44$

Day 48

1) $14 + (6 + (5 + 2)^2)$
  $14 + (6 + \quad 7^2 \quad)$
  $14 + (6 + \quad 49 \quad)$
  $14 + \qquad 55$
  $\qquad 69$

2) $10 + ((18 + 4) + 3^2)$
  $10 + (\quad 22 \quad + 3^2)$
  $10 + (\quad 22 \quad + 9)$
  $10 + \qquad 31$
  $\qquad 41$

3) $14 + ((15 - 3) \times 5^2)$
  $14 + (\quad 12 \quad \times 5^2)$
  $14 + (\quad 12 \quad \times 25)$
  $14 + \qquad 300$
  $\qquad 314$

4) $((6 + 4)^2 + 6) - 4^2$
  $(\quad 10^2 \quad + 6) - 4^2$
  $(\quad 100 \quad + 6) - 4^2$
  $\qquad 106 \quad - 4^2$
  $\qquad 106 \quad - 16$
  $\qquad 90$

5) $19 + (9 + (9 - 5)^2)$
  $19 + (9 + \quad 4^2 \quad)$
  $19 + (9 + \quad 16 \quad)$
  $10 + \quad 25$
  $\qquad 44$

6) $((10 - 4) + (14 - 7)^2)$
  $(\quad 6 \quad + (\quad 7 \quad)^2)$
  $(\quad 6 \quad + \quad 49 \quad)$
  $\qquad 55$

7) $(3^2 + (24 - 3 + 2^2))$
  $(3^2 + (24 - 3 + 4))$
  $(3^2 + (\quad 21 \quad + 4))$
  $(3^2 + \qquad 25 \quad)$
  $(9 + \qquad 25 \quad)$
  $\qquad 34$

8) $((11 - 4)^2 \times 7) - 4^2$
  $(\quad 7^2 \quad \times 7) - 4^2$
  $(\quad 49 \quad \times 7) - 4^2$
  $\qquad 343 \qquad - 4^2$
  $\qquad 343 \qquad - 16$
  $\qquad 327$

9) $((9 - 7) + (16 - 8)^2)$
  $(\quad 2 \quad + (\quad 8 \quad)^2)$
  $(\quad 2 \quad + \quad 64 \quad)$
  $\qquad 66$

10) $(6^2 + (10 - 2 + 3^2))$
  $(6^2 + (10 - 2 + 9))$
  $(6^2 + (\quad 8 \quad + 9))$
  $(6^2 + \qquad 17 \quad)$
  $(36 + \qquad 17 \quad)$
  $\qquad 53$

Day 49

1) $(4^2 + (12 - 3 + 3^2))$
   $(4^2 + (12 - 3 + 9))$
   $(4^2 + (9 + 9))$
   $(4^2 + 18)$
   $(16 + 18)$
       34

2) $((11 + 4) + (8 - 2)^2)$
   $(15 + (6)^2)$
   $(15 + 36)$
           51

3) $((11 - 3)^2 \times 6) + 3^2$
   $(8^2 \times 6) + 3^2$
   $(64 \times 6) + 3^2$
       384 $+ 3^2$
       384 + 9
           393

4) $((12 - 4) + (16 - 2)^2)$
   $(8 + (14)^2)$
   $(8 + 196)$
       204

5) $(3^2 + (8 - 4 + 4^2))$
   $(3^2 + (8 - 4 + 16))$
   $(3^2 + (4 + 16))$
   $(3^2 + 20)$
   $(9 + 20)$
       29

6) $14 + ((17 - 6) \times 3^2)$
   $14 + (11 \times 3^2)$
   $14 + (11 \times 9)$
   $14 + 99$
           113

7) $15 + ((9 + 3) + 3^2)$
   $15 + (12 + 3^2)$
   $15 + (12 + 9)$
   $15 + 21$
           36

8) $((5 + 4)^2 + 4) - 3^2$
   $(9^2 + 4) - 3^2$
   $(81 + 4) - 3^2$
           85 $- 3^2$
           85 - 9
               76

9) $5 + (8 + (11 - 4)^2)$
   $5 + (8 + 7^2)$
   $5 + (8 + 49)$
   $5 + 57$
           62

10) $7 + (6 + (9 - 4)^2)$
   $7 + (6 + 5^2)$
   $7 + (6 + 25)$
   $7 + 31$
           38

Day 50

1) $((5 + 2)^2 \times 3) - 2^2$
    $(\quad 7^2 \quad \times 3) - 2^2$
    $(\quad 49 \quad \times 3) - 2^2$
    $\qquad 147 \qquad - 2^2$
    $\qquad 147 \qquad - 4$
    $\qquad\qquad 143$

2) $((12 + 7) + (15 - 3)^2)$
    $(\quad 19 \quad + (\quad 12 \quad)^2)$
    $(\quad 19 \quad + \quad 144 \quad)$
    $\qquad\qquad 163$

3) $13 + (5 \times (6 + 3)^2)$
    $13 + (5 \times \quad 9^2 \quad)$
    $13 + (5 \times \quad 81 \quad)$
    $13 + \quad 405$
    $\qquad\qquad 418$

4) $(5^2 + (10 - 5 + 3^2))$
    $(5^2 + (10 - 5 + 9))$
    $(5^2 + (5 \quad + 9))$
    $(5^2 + \qquad 14 \quad)$
    $(25 + \qquad 14 \quad)$
    $\qquad\quad 39$

5) $20 + ((18 + 7) \times 5^2)$
    $20 + (\quad 25 \quad \times 5^2)$
    $20 + (\quad 25 \quad \times 25)$
    $20 + \qquad 625$
    $\qquad\qquad 645$

6) $24 + ((10 + 3) + 3^2)$
    $24 + (\qquad 13 \quad + 3^2)$
    $24 + (\qquad 13 \quad + 9)$
    $24 + \qquad 22$
    $\qquad\qquad 46$

7) $(5^2 + (8 - 2 + 3^2))$
    $(5^2 + (8 - 2 + 9))$
    $(5^2 + (6 \quad + 9))$
    $(5^2 + \qquad 15 \quad)$
    $(25 + \qquad 15 \quad)$
    $\qquad\quad 40$

8) $((14 - 2) + (16 - 2)^2)$
    $(\quad 12 \quad + (\quad 14 \quad)^2)$
    $(\quad 12 \quad + \quad 196 \quad)$
    $\qquad\quad 208$

9) $6 + (10 \times (4 + 6)^2)$
    $6 + (10 \times \quad 10^2 \quad)$
    $6 + (10 \times \quad 100 \quad)$
    $6 +$
    $\qquad 1006$

10) $((5 + 3)^2 + 6) + 2^2$
    $(\quad 8^2 \quad + 6) + 2^2$
    $(\quad 64 \quad + 6) + 2^2$
    $\qquad 70 \qquad + 2^2$
    $\qquad 70 \qquad + 4$
    $\qquad\qquad 74$

Day 51

1) 14 - 3 x 7 + 16 - 8
    14 -   21 + 16 - 8
                  1

2) 4 - 2 + 4 x 8 + 19
    4 - 2 +   32 + 19
             53

3) 5 x 14 + 10 x 16 + 9
    70 + 10 x 16 + 9
    70 +   160 + 9
          239

4) 9 + 2 x 5 - 4 - 2
    9 +   10 - 4 - 2
          13

5) 6 x 7 x 2 - 1 - 1
    42 x 2 - 1 - 1
    84 - 1 - 1
       82

6) 9 - 1 + 15 - 13 x 12
    9 - 1 + 15 -   156
          -133

7) 18 x 6 + 18 + 19 x 4
    108 + 18 + 19 x 4
    108 + 18 +   76
        202

8) 9 x 10 + 11 - 11 - 10
    90 + 11 - 11 - 10
        80

9) 19 + 10 - 6 - 4 x 17
    19 + 10 - 6 -   68
        -45

10) 2 - 1 x 19 x 12 + 6
    2 -   19 x 12 + 6
    2 -   228 + 6
       -220

Day 52

1) 16 - 6 x 11 + 14 - 14
   16 -   66 + 14 - 14
              -50

2) 15 x 18 - 9 - 8 + 9
    270 - 9 - 8 + 9
            262

3) 2 x 17 - 11 + 4 x 7
    34 - 11 + 4 x 7
    34 - 11 +   28
           51

4) 16 x 3 + 9 x 12 - 5
    48 + 9 x 12 - 5
    48 +   108 - 5
          151

5) 16 - 15 x 13 x 17 + 4
   16 -   195 x 17 + 4
   16 -   3315 + 4
       3206

6) 11 x 16 x 2 - 1 + 3
    176 x 2 - 1 + 3
    352 - 1 + 3
       354

7) 8 + 10 - 8 x 2 x 7
   8 + 10 -   16 x 7
   8 + 10 -   112
       -94

8) 5 x 11 - 9 x 3 + 7
   55 - 9 x 3 + 7
   55 -   27 + 7
       35

9) 14 x 12 - 4 - 1 + 5
   168 - 4 - 1 + 5
      168

10) 4 - 3 - 1 x 2 + 15
   4 - 3 -   2 + 15
      14

Day 53

1) 9 - 1 + 11 + 13 x 19
    9 - 1 + 11 +   247
              266

2) 2 - 1 + 13 x 19 + 7
    2 - 1 +   247 + 7
             255

3) 15 x 19 + 11 - 7 + 12
    285 + 11 - 7 + 12
             301

4) 10 - 7 x 4 + 3 - 2
    10 -   28 + 3 - 2
             -17

5) 19 - 7 x 4 + 15 + 6
    19 -   28 + 15 + 6
             12

6) 12 + 11 x 4 - 3 - 1
    12 +   44 - 3 - 1
             52

7) 12 - 10 + 3 x 9 + 8
    12 - 10 +   27 + 8
             37

8) 13 + 5 x 17 - 12 + 4
    13 +   85 - 12 + 4
             90

9) 17 x 6 - 6 + 7 x 9
    102 - 6 + 7 x 9
    102 - 6 +   63
             159

10) 13 x 14 - 11 + 5 x 11
    182 - 11 + 5 x 11
    182 - 11 +   55
             226

Day 54

1) 10 x 14 - 9 + 17 + 5
    140 - 9 + 17 + 5
             153

2) 2 + 3 + 7 - 2 x 14
    2 + 3 + 7 -   28
            -16

3) 16 + 5 x 15 - 2 + 19
    16 +   75 - 2 + 19
            108

4) 8 - 5 + 3 x 16 x 8
    8 - 5 +   48 x 8
    8 - 5 +   384
          387

5) 16 + 5 - 3 + 6 - 5
          19

6) 2 + 4 - 3 - 1 x 2
    2 + 4 - 3 -   2
          1

7) 19 + 3 + 18 - 9 - 5
          26

8) 13 x 13 - 3 x 8 + 8
    169 - 3 x 8 + 8
    169 -   24 + 8
          153

9) 14 + 12 + 12 - 10 x 12
    14 + 12 + 12 -   120
          -82

10) 17 - 3 x 7 + 6 + 9
    17 -   21 + 6 + 9
          11

Day 55

1) 13 - 6 x 19 + 5 - 3
    13 -   114 + 5 - 3
               -99

2) 3 +10 +12 - 11 x 10
    3 + 10 + 12 -   110
              -85

3) 15 x 15 - 13 + 3 +19
    225 - 13 + 3 + 19
           234

4) 8 x 17 +10 + 4 - 2
    136 + 10 + 4 - 2
           148

5) 18 + 7 x 7 - 4 - 4
    18 +   49 - 4 - 4
          59

6) 5 - 3 +15 - 9 + 7
             15

7) 19 - 15 x 11 + 9 x 7
    19 -   165 + 9 x 7
    19 -   165 +   63
           -83

8) 13 - 5 + 5 +10 x 14
    13 - 5 + 5 +   140
            153

9) 9 - 3 + 5 x 11 - 10
    9 - 3 +   55 - 10
           51

10) 5 + 8 - 2 x 14 - 11
    5 + 8 -   28 - 11
          -26

Day 56

1) 2 + 13 - 2 x 10 + 2
     2 + 13 -   20 + 2
                          -3

2) 10 - 4 + 7 + 19 x 5
     10 - 4 + 7 +   95
                        108

3) 8 + 2 x 12 x 14 - 10
     8 +   24 x 14 - 10
     8 +   336 - 10
                        334

4) 19 x 4 + 9 x 17 - 12
     76 + 9 x 17 - 12
     76 +   153 - 12
                    217

5) 5 - 1 + 11 + 5 x 5
     5 - 1 + 11 +   25
                          40

6) 11 - 4 + 19 x 2 - 1
     11 - 4 +   38 - 1
                          44

7) 14 x 4 x 9 - 2 + 5
     56 x 9 - 2 + 5
     504 - 2 + 5
                    507

8) 13 + 19 x 14 x 18 + 15
     13 +   266 x 18 + 15
     13 +   4788 + 15
                        4816

9) 19 + 4 x 2 - 1 + 18
     19 +   8 - 1 + 18
                          44

10) 7 + 9 - 8 x 13 - 7
      7 + 9 -   104 - 7
                        -95

Day 57

1) 14 + 5 x 16 + 7 x 12
   14 +   80 + 7 x 12
   14 +   80 +   84
                          178

2) 12 + 2 x 17 - 16 x 14
   12 +   34 - 16 x 14
   12 +   34 -   224
                         -178

3) 19 - 2 +11 x 12 x 3
   19 - 2 +   132 x 3
   19 - 2 +   396
                         413

4) 7 + 7 - 4 x 9 x 18
   7 + 7 -   36 x 18
   7 + 7 -   648
                        -634

5) 2 + 4 x 7 - 5 - 1
   2 +   28 - 5 - 1
                        24

6) 12 x 19 - 7 +11 x 10
   228 - 7 + 11 x 10
   228 - 7 +   110
                         331

7) 17 x 5 - 4 + 5 - 2
   85 - 4 + 5 - 2
                        84

8) 7 x 16 + 8 + 9 x 11
   112 + 8 + 9 x 11
   112 + 8 +   99
                         219

9) 12 x 10 x 7 + 9 +15
   120 x 7 + 9 + 15
   840 + 9 + 15
                         864

10) 13 - 6 + 6 - 1 x 14
    13 - 6 + 6 -   14
                          -1

Day 58

1) 3 + 15 - 4 x 18 - 5
     3 + 15 -   72 - 5
                    -59

2) 12 + 13 - 6 x 11 - 4
     12 + 13 -   66 - 4
                      -45

3) 5 - 2 + 5 + 10 - 6
                        12

4) 17 x 18 + 3 - 2 x 4
     306 + 3 - 2 x 4
     306 + 3 -   8
                      301

5) 7 x 10 - 10 + 8 - 3
     70 - 10 + 8 - 3
                    65

6) 10 x 17 - 12 + 4 - 4
     170 - 12 + 4 - 4
                       158

7) 10 - 4 + 15 - 10 x 13
     10 - 4 + 15 -   130
                      -109

8) 18 + 5 x 12 - 12 + 14
     18 +   60 - 12 + 14
                        80

9) 7 + 7 + 12 - 6 x 14
     7 + 7 + 12 -   84
                      -58

10) 3 + 16 - 2 x 13 - 3
      3 + 16 -   26 - 3
                        -10

Day 59

1) 16 - 4 x 13 x 18 + 13
    16 -   52 x 18 + 13
    16 -   936 + 13
                      -907

2) 11 - 5 x 5 - 4 + 9
    11 -   25 - 4 + 9
                    -9

3) 6 x 2 x 4 + 2 + 16
    12 x 4 + 2 + 16
        48 + 2 + 16
              66

4) 11 + 8 - 6 + 15 x 17
    11 + 8 - 6 +   255
                 268

5) 3 + 4 - 1 + 10 x 11
    3 + 4 - 1 +   110
              116

6) 6 x 7 + 11 x 19 - 17
    42 + 11 x 19 - 17
    42 +   209 - 17
              234

7) 17 x 2 + 13 + 12 x 15
    34 + 13 + 12 x 15
    34 + 13 +   180
              227

8) 9 - 2 - 1 x 12 + 14
    9 - 2 -   12 + 14
                    9

9) 7 - 5 + 3 x 3 + 8
    7 - 5 +   9 + 8
               19

10) 19 - 13 + 17 - 11 x 14
     19 - 13 + 17 -   154
                  -131

Day 60

1) 16 - 12 + 15 + 19 x 4
    16 - 12 + 15 +   76
                      95

2) 6 - 2 + 10 x 16 - 7
    6 - 2 +   160 - 7
                157

3) 16 + 6 x 13 x 9 - 6
   16 +   78 x 9 - 6
   16 +   702 - 6
            712

4) 2 + 15 - 5 x 11 - 5
   2 + 15 -   55 - 5
            -43

5) 6 + 6 - 4 x 8 x 9
   6 + 6 -   32 x 9
   6 + 6 -   288
          -276

6) 18 + 16 + 6 x 14 - 2
   18 + 16 +   84 - 2
              116

7) 4 x 13 x 18 + 19 - 4
    52 x 18 + 19 - 4
     936 + 19 - 4
          951

8) 14 x 6 - 3 - 1 + 15
     84 - 3 - 1 + 15
           95

9) 9 + 13 - 3 + 14 x 13
   9 + 13 - 3 +   182
            201

10) 9 - 9 + 18 x 5 - 2
   9 - 9 +   90 - 2
           88

Day 61

1) (10 - 5) x (12 + 4) + 4
     5   x   16   + 4
       80   + 4
                84

2) (9 +45 - 4) + 5 + 7
  (54   - 4) + 5 + 7
     50   + 5 + 7
        55   + 7
            62

3) (10 +35 - 5) - (15 - 5)
  (45   - 5) -   10
     40   -   10
         30

4) (12 - 5) x (10 +10 - 5)
     7   x (10 +   5)
     7   x   15
       105

5) (14 +20 - 6) + 4 + 7
  (34   - 6) + 4 + 7
     28   + 4 + 7
       32 + 7
         39

6) (17 - 3) x (14 + 4) +10
   14   x   18   +10
      252   +10
         262

7) 7 x (11 x 4 +10) - 3
   7 x (44   +10) - 3
   7 x   54   - 3
     378   - 3
       375

8) (14 - 2) x (6 +12 - 3)
   12   x (6 +   9)
   12   x   15
      180

9) 5 x (2 x 6 + 9) - 9
   5 x (12   + 9) - 9
   5 x   21   - 9
     105   - 9
       96

10) (12 +17 - 5) - (2 + 2)
  (29   - 5) -   4
     24   -   4
       20

Day 62

1) (8 + 4) x (10 +15 - 3)
    12   x (10 +   12   )
    12   x   22
            264

2) (8 +45 - 3) - (27 - 2)
    (53   - 3) -   25
      50   -   25
                25

3) (21 - 3) x (13 + 6) - 7
    18   x   19   - 7
      342   - 7
              335

4) (8 +42 - 2) + 6 + 2
    (50   - 2) + 6 + 2
       48   + 6 + 2
         54   + 2
            56

5) (10 - 3) x (6 +10 - 2)
    7   x (6 +   8   )
    7   x   14
          98

6)   2 x (13 x   9 + 5) - 8
    2 x (117   + 5) - 8
    2 x   - 8
        244   - 8
                 236

7) (10 +43 - 3) - (27 - 2)
    (53   - 3) -   25
      50   -   25
                25

8)   2 x (13 x   8 - 8) + 6
    2 x (104   - 8) + 6
    2 x   96   + 6
       192   + 6
                198

9) (14 +19 - 5) + 2 + 4
    (33   - 5) + 2 + 4
       28   + 2 + 4
         30   + 4
            34

10) (10 - 7) x (12 + 6) - 3
    3   x   18   - 3
       54   - 3
              51

Day 63

1) (9 +21 - 6) + 6 + 5
  (30   - 6) + 6 + 5
        24   + 6 + 5
            30   + 5
                35

2) (8 +29 - 5) - (2 + 6)
  (37   - 5) -   8
        32   -   8
                24

3) (13 + 4) x (12 + 6) + 8
      17   x   18   + 8
          306   + 8
                    314

4)   8 x (6 x 10 + 8) + 10
      8 x (60   + 8) + 10
      8 x   68   + 10
          544   + 10
                    554

5)   7 x (8 x   9 - 10) + 10
      7 x (72   - 10) + 10
      7 x   62   + 10
          434   + 10
                    444

6) (14 +40 - 6) - (-3 + 6)
  (54   - 6) -   3
        48   -   3
                45

7) (14 - 4) x (10 +12 - 4)
      10   x (10 +   8   )
      10   x   18
                180

8) (14 - 3) x (7 +10 - 5)
      11   x (7 +   5   )
      11   x   12
                132

9) (12 +24 - 4) + 16 + 2
  (36   - 4) + 16 + 2
        32   + 16 + 2
            48   + 2
                50

10) (14 + 2) x (13 - 2) - 7
      16   x   11   - 7
          176   - 7
                    169

Day 64

1) (10 + 31 - 5) + 18 - 3
　　(41 - 5) + 18 - 3
　　　36 　　+ 18 - 3
　　　　　 54 　- 3
　　　　　　　 51

2) (9 + 43 - 4) - (6 + 2)
　　(52 - 4) - 　 8
　　　48 　- 　 8
　　　　　　 40

3) (9 + 32 - 5) - (1 + 3)
　　(41 - 5) - 　 4
　　　36 　- 　 4
　　　　　　 32

4) (10 + 6) x (9 - 6) + 9
　　　16 　 x 　 3 　+ 9
　　　　 48 　　+ 9
　　　　　　　 57

5) (13 - 5) x (8 + 4) - 5
　　　 8 　 x 　12 　- 5
　　　　 96 　　- 5
　　　　　　　 91

6) (15 + 2) x (9 + 12 - 2)
　　　17 　 x (9 + 　10 　)
　　　17 　 x 　 19
　　　　　　 323

7) (14 + 37 - 3) + 12 + 4
　　(51 - 3) + 12 + 4
　　　　48 　　+ 12 + 4
　　　　　　 60 　+ 4
　　　　　　　　 64

8) 10 x (10 x 5 - 4) + 8
　　10 x (50 　- 4) + 8
　　10 x 　 46 　　+ 8
　　　　 460 　　+ 8
　　　　　　　 468

9) 4 x (7 x 6 - 7) + 5
　　4 x (42 　- 7) + 5
　　4 x 　 35 　　+ 5
　　　 140 　　+ 5
　　　　　　 145

10) (15 - 3) x (14 + 10 - 5)
　　　12 　 x (14 + 　 5 　)
　　　12 　 x 　 19
　　　　　　 228

Day 65

1) (16 - 2) x (7 + 12 - 6)
      14   x (7 +   6)
      14   x   13
                              182

2)   4 x (11 x 2 - 8) + 7
       4 x (22   - 8) + 7
       4 x   14   + 7
              56   + 7
                              63

3) (15 + 21 - 6) + 2 - 5
     (36   - 6) + 2 - 5
            30   + 2 - 5
                  32   - 5
                              27

4) (8 + 33 - 5) + 6 - 3
     (41   - 5) + 6 - 3
            36   + 6 - 3
                  42   - 3
                              39

5) (16 + 5) x (10 + 18 - 9)
       21   x (10 +   9)
       21   x   19
                              399

6) (14 + 28 - 2) - (16 + 4)
     (42   - 2) -   20
            40   -   20
                              20

7) (17 - 5) x (8 + 4) - 3
       12   x   12   - 3
                  144   - 3
                              141

8) (20 + 8) x (8 + 6) + 10
       28   x   14   + 10
                  392   + 10
                              402

9)   7 x (9 x 5 + 7) - 5
       7 x (45   + 7) - 5
       7 x   52   - 5
              364   - 5
                              359

10) (10 + 34 - 4) - (10 - 2)
      (44   - 4) -   8
             40   -   8
                              32

Day 66

1) (14 + 5) x (12 + 2) + 6
      19   x   14   + 6
             266   + 6
                             272

2)   7 x (5 x 6 - 7) + 4
      7 x (30   - 7) + 4
      7 x   23   + 4
             161   + 4
                          165

3) (16 - 6) x (11 + 6) - 10
      10   x   17   - 10
             170   - 10
                           160

4)   5 x (6 x 5 + 5) - 6
      5 x (30   + 5) - 6
      5 x   35   - 6
             175   - 6
                          169

5) (14 + 19 - 3) - (6 - 3)
      (33   - 3) -   3
             30   -   3
                            27

6) (8 - 4) x (13 + 18 - 6)
      4   x (13 +   12   )
      4   x   25
                   100

7) (14 + 21 - 5) + 2 - 7
      (35   - 5) + 2 - 7
             30   + 2 - 7
                    32   - 7
                          25

8) (8 - 4) x (11 + 24 - 2)
      4   x (11 +   22   )
      4   x   33
                   132

9) (11 + 26 - 5) + 8 + 3
      (37   - 5) + 8 + 3
             32   + 8 + 3
                    40   + 3
                          43

10) (10 + 26 - 6) - (-3 + 6)
      (36   - 6) -   3
             30   -   3
                            27

Day 67

1) (14 + 22 - 6) + 2 + 6
   (36 - 6) + 2 + 6
     30   + 2 + 6
       32 + 6
         38

2) (16 + 5) x (6 + 16 - 2)
   21   x (6 + 14)
   21   x   20
      420

3) (12 + 21 - 5) - (-1 + 3)
   (33 - 5) - 2
     28   - 2
       26

4) 3 x (11 x 10 + 9) + 10
   3 x (110   + 9) + 10
   3 x   + 10
    357   + 10
      367

5) (13 - 4) x (9 + 2) - 8
   9   x 11 - 8
    99   - 8
     91

6) (9 + 26 - 5) - (5 - 2)
   (35 - 5) - 3
    30   - 3
     27

7) 8 x (13 x 8 + 3) + 7
   8 x (104 + 3) + 7
   8 x   + 7
    856   + 7
     863

8) (11 + 2) x (6 + 18 - 3)
   13   x (6 + 15)
   13   x 21
    273

9) (11 + 31 - 6) + 2 + 5
   (42 - 6) + 2 + 5
    36   + 2 + 5
     38 + 5
      43

10) (15 - 4) x (9 + 6) - 10
   11   x 15 - 10
    165 - 10
     155

Day 68

1) $(16 + 5) \times (9 + 2) - 2$
$\ 21 \quad \times \quad 11 \quad - 2$
$\qquad 231 \qquad\quad - 2$
$\qquad\qquad\qquad\quad 229$

2) $(11 - 2) \times (10 - 2) + 10$
$\quad 9 \quad \times \quad 8 \quad + 10$
$\qquad 72 \qquad\quad + 10$
$\qquad\qquad\qquad\quad 82$

3) $5 \times (13 \times 6 - 3) + 2$
$\ 5 \times (\ 78 \qquad - 3) + 2$
$\ 5 \times \qquad 75 \qquad + 2$
$\qquad 375 \qquad\qquad + 2$
$\qquad\qquad\qquad\qquad 377$

4) $(13 + 41 - 4) - (2 + 3)$
$\ (\ 54 \quad - 4) - \quad 5$
$\qquad 50 \qquad - \quad 5$
$\qquad\qquad\qquad\quad 45$

5) $6 \times (4 \times 2 + 9) + 10$
$\ 6 \times (\ 8 \qquad + 9) + 10$
$\ 6 \times \qquad 17 \qquad + 10$
$\qquad 102 \qquad\qquad + 10$
$\qquad\qquad\qquad 112$

6) $(13 + 4) \times (8 + 15 - 3)$
$\qquad 17 \quad \times (8 + \quad 12 \quad)$
$\qquad 17 \quad \times \quad 20$
$\qquad\qquad\quad 340$

7) $(15 + 17 - 4) + 2 + 7$
$\ (\ 32 \quad - 4) + 2 + 7$
$\qquad 28 \qquad + 2 + 7$
$\qquad\qquad 30 \quad + 7$
$\qquad\qquad\qquad 37$

8) $(15 + 31 - 6) - (1 + 7)$
$\ (\ 46 \quad - 6) - \quad 8$
$\qquad 40 \qquad - \quad 8$
$\qquad\qquad\qquad 32$

9) $(14 + 32 - 6) + 20 + 6$
$\ (\ 46 \quad - 6) + 20 + 6$
$\qquad 40 \qquad + 20 + 6$
$\qquad\qquad 60 \quad + 6$
$\qquad\qquad\qquad 66$

10) $(13 - 3) \times (11 + 10 - 5)$
$\quad 10 \quad \times (11 + \quad 5 \quad)$
$\quad 10 \quad \times \quad 16$
$\qquad\qquad 160$

Day 69

1) (20 + 4) x (8 - 2) - 3
   24   x   6   - 3
        144   - 3
                    141

2) (13 +52 - 5) - (-1 + 6)
   (65   - 5) -   5
        60   -   5
                      55

3) (9 - 3) x (14 +18 - 2)
      6   x (14 +   16)
      6   x   30
            180

4) (10 +44 - 6) - (-1 + 4)
   (54   - 6) -   3
        48   -   3
                     45

5) (9 + 5) x (9 +24 - 6)
      14   x (9 +   18)
      14   x   27
            378

6) (16 - 3) x (12 + 2) +10
   13   x   14   +10
        182   +10
                   192

7) (13 +29 - 6) + 3 + 2
   (42   - 6) + 3 + 2
        36   + 3 + 2
            39   + 2
                 41

8) (14 +31 - 5) + 5 - 3
   (45   - 5) + 5 - 3
        40   + 5 - 3
            45   - 3
                 42

9) 5 x (3 x 10 - 4) - 9
     5 x (30   - 4) - 9
     5 x   26   - 9
           130   - 9
                      121

10) 9 x (11 x 9 - 6) +10
      9 x (99   - 6) +10
      9 x   93   +10
            837   +10
                      847

Day 70

1) (10 +42 - 2) +25 + 7
   (52 - 2) +25 + 7
     50   +25 + 7
        75   + 7
          82

2) (15 + 4) x (15 + 8 - 4)
    19   x (15 + 4)
    19   x   19
       361

3) (11 +52 - 3) + 5 - 5
   (63 - 3) + 5 - 5
     60   + 5 - 5
       65 - 5
        60

4) 3 x (7 x 3 + 8) - 10
   3 x (21 + 8) - 10
   3 x   29   - 10
     87   - 10
       77

5) (17 + 2) x (12 + 3) - 4
    19   x   15 - 4
    285   - 4
     281

6) 2 x (10 x 7 - 4) - 6
   2 x (70 - 4) - 6
   2 x   66   - 6
    132   - 6
     126

7) (9 +22 - 3) - (-4 + 6)
   (31 - 3) -   2
    28   -   2
     26

8) (10 +41 - 3) - (14 - 2)
   (51 - 3) -   12
    48   -   12
     36

9) (10 + 4) x (11 + 5) - 7
    14   x   16 - 7
    224   - 7
     217

10) (13 + 5) x (9 +10 - 2)
    18   x (9 + 8)
    18   x   17
     306

Day 71

1) $8 \times (6 \times 4 - 6^2) - 8$
$8 \times (6 \times 4 - 36) - 8$
$8 \times (24 \quad - 36) - 8$
$8 \times \quad -12 \quad\quad - 8$
$\quad -96 \quad\quad\quad - 8$
$\quad\quad\quad\quad -104$

2) $(14 + 19 - 3) - 15 - 2^2$
$(14 + 19 - 3) - 15 - 4$
$(\quad 33 \quad - 3) - 15 - 4$
$30 \quad\quad - 15 - 4$
$\quad\quad 15 \quad - 4$
$\quad\quad\quad\quad 11$

3) $(12 + 31 - 3) - 10 - 4^2$
$(12 + 31 - 3) - 10 - 16$
$(\quad 43 \quad - 3) - 10 - 16$
$40 \quad\quad - 10 - 16$
$\quad\quad 30 \quad - 16$
$\quad\quad\quad 14$

4) $(6 + 4)^2 + (12 + 18 + 9)$
$(\quad 10 \quad)^2 + (12 + \quad 27 \quad)$
$100 \quad + \quad 39$
$\quad\quad\quad 139$

5) $(19 - 7) \times (11 - 5) + 2^2$
$(19 - 7) \times (11 - 5) + 4$
$12 \quad \times \quad 6 \quad + 4$
$\quad 72 \quad\quad + 4$
$\quad\quad\quad 76$

6) $(14 + 46 - 6^2) + (5 - 2)$
$(14 + 46 - 36) + (5 - 2)$
$(\quad 60 \quad - 36) + \quad 3$
$24 \quad\quad + \quad 3$
$\quad\quad\quad 27$

7) $(17 + 6) \times (8 - 3) + 9^2$
$(17 + 6) \times (8 - 3) + 81$
$23 \quad \times \quad 5 \quad + 81$
$\quad 115 \quad\quad + 81$
$\quad\quad\quad\quad 196$

8) $(14 - 5)^2 + (16 + 10 + 2)$
$(\quad 9 \quad)^2 + (16 + \quad 12 \quad)$
$81 \quad + \quad\quad 28$
$\quad\quad\quad 109$

9) $4 \times (8 \times 10 + 7^2) - 3$
$4 \times (8 \times 10 + 49) - 3$
$4 \times (80 \quad + 49) - 3$
$4 \times \quad 129 \quad\quad - 3$
$\quad 516 \quad\quad\quad - 3$
$\quad\quad\quad\quad 513$

10) $(10 + 65 - 5^2) + (8 - 6)$
$(10 + 65 - 25) + (8 - 6)$
$(\quad 75 \quad - 25) + \quad 2$
$50 \quad\quad + \quad 2$
$\quad\quad\quad 52$

Day 72

1) $(17 + 2)$ x $(12 + 6)$ - 6^2
$(17 + 2)$ x $(12 + 6)$ - 36
19   x   18   - 36
342   - 36
306

6) $(10 + 5)^2 + (15 + 12 + 4)$
$(\quad 15 \quad)^2 + (15 + \quad 16 \quad)$
225   +   31
256

2) $(6 + 2)^2 + (13 + 10 - 5)$
$(\quad 8 \quad)^2 + (13 + \quad 5 \quad)$
64   +   18
82

7) $(9 + 44 - 5^2) + (1 + 6)$
$(9 + 44 - 25) + (1 + 6)$
$(\quad 53 \quad - 25) + \quad 7$
28   +   7
35

3) 5 x $(3$ x $7 + 2^2) + 10$
5 x $(3$ x $7 + 4) + 10$
5 x $(21 \quad + 4) + 10$
5 x   25   +10
125   +10
135

8) 9 x $(13$ x $2 + 4^2) + 10$
9 x $(13$ x $2 + 16) + 10$
9 x $(26 \quad + 16) + 10$
9 x   42   +10
378   +10
388

4) $(13 + 18 - 3) - 4 + 4^2$
$(13 + 18 - 3) - 4 + 16$
$(\quad 31 \quad - 3) - 4 + 16$
28   - 4 + 16
24   +16
40

9) $(11 + 42 - 5) - 3 - 5^2$
$(11 + 42 - 5) - 3 - 25$
$(\quad 53 \quad - 5) - 3 - 25$
48   - 3 - 25
45   - 25
20

5) $(12 + 40 - 2^2) + (1 + 7)$
$(12 + 40 - 4) + (1 + 7)$
$(\quad 52 \quad - 4) + \quad 8$
48   +   8
50

10) $(20 + 2)$ x $(12 - 3) - 3^2$
$(20 + 2)$ x $(12 - 3) - 9$
22   x   9   - 9
198   9

Day 73

1) $(15 + 17 - 2) - 10 + 3^2$
$(15 + 17 - 2) - 10 + 9$
$(\quad 32 \quad - 2) - 10 + 9$
$\qquad 30 \qquad - 10 + 9$
$\qquad\qquad 20 \quad + 9$
$\qquad\qquad\qquad 29$

2) $4 \times (11 \times 5 + 7^2) + 3$
$4 \times (11 \times 5 + 49) + 3$
$4 \times (\quad 55 \qquad + 49) + 3$
$4 \times \qquad 104 \qquad + 3$
$\qquad 416 \qquad\qquad + 3$
$\qquad\qquad\qquad 419$

3) $(12 + 38 - 2) - 8 + 6^2$
$(12 + 38 - 2) - 8 + 36$
$(\quad 50 \quad - 2) - 8 + 36$
$\qquad 48 \qquad - 8 + 36$
$\qquad\qquad 40 \quad + 36$
$\qquad\qquad\qquad 76$

4) $(17 + 6) \times (13 + 6) - 9^2$
$(17 + 6) \times (13 + 6) - 81$
$\qquad 23 \qquad \times \quad 19 \quad - 81$
$\qquad\qquad 437 \qquad - 81$
$\qquad\qquad\qquad 356$

5) $(16 - 7) \times (13 + 6) - 9^2$
$(16 - 7) \times (13 + 6) - 81$
$\qquad 9 \qquad \times \quad 19 \quad - 81$
$\qquad\qquad 171 \qquad - 81$
$\qquad\qquad\qquad 90$

6) $(13 + 41 - 2^2) + (12 - 2)$
$(13 + 41 - 4 \quad) + (12 - 2)$
$(\quad 54 \quad - 4) + \quad 10$
$\qquad 50 \qquad + \quad 10$
$\qquad\qquad\qquad 60$

7) $(2 + 3)^2 + (12 + 20 - 4)$
$(\quad 5 \quad)^2 + (12 + \quad 16 \quad)$
$\qquad 25 \quad + \qquad 28$
$\qquad\qquad\qquad 53$

8) $(5 + 4)^2 + (15 + 12 - 6)$
$(\quad 9 \quad)^2 + (15 + \quad 6 \quad)$
$\qquad 81 \quad + \qquad 21$
$\qquad\qquad\qquad 102$

9) $(11 + 53 - 6^2) + (3 + 4)$
$(11 + 53 - 36 \quad) + (3 + 4)$
$(\quad 64 \quad - 36) + \quad 7$
$\qquad 28 \qquad + \quad 7$
$\qquad\qquad\qquad 35$

10) $2 \times (10 \times 6 - 2^2) + 5$
$2 \times (10 \times 6 - 4 \quad) + 5$
$2 \times (\quad 60 \qquad - 4) + 5$
$2 \times \qquad 56 \qquad\qquad + 5$
$\qquad 112 \qquad\qquad + 5$
$\qquad\qquad\qquad 117$

Day 74

1) $(15 + 40 - 5^2) + (4 + 6)$
$(15 + 40 - 25) + (4 + 6)$
$(55 - 25) + 10$
$30 + 10$
40

2) $(10 + 3)^2 + (12 + 8 - 4)$
$(13)^2 + (12 + 4)$
$169 + 16$
185

3) $7 \times (13 \times 10 - 4^2) + 9$
$7 \times (13 \times 10 - 16) + 9$
$7 \times (130 - 16) + 9$
$7 \times 114 + 9$
$798 + 9$
807

4) $(15 + 33 - 4^2) + (19 - 3)$
$(15 + 33 - 16) + (19 - 3)$
$(48 - 16) + 16$
$32 + 16$
48

5) $(20 - 3) \times (14 + 5) - 5^2$
$(20 - 3) \times (14 + 5) - 25$
$17 \times 19 - 25$
$323 \quad 25$
290

6) $(13 - 5)^2 + (15 + 12 + 3)$
$(8)^2 + (15 + 15)$
$64 + 30$
94

7) $(15 + 38 - 3) - 5 + 2^2$
$(15 + 38 - 3) - 5 + 4$
$(53 - 3) - 5 + 4$
$50 - 5 + 4$
$45 + 4$
49

8) $(10 + 32 - 6) - 9 - 7^2$
$(10 + 32 - 6) - 9 - 49$
$(42 - 6) - 9 - 49$
$36 - 9 - 49$
$27 - 49$
-22

9) $(14 + 2) \times (12 - 4) - 2^2$
$(14 + 2) \times (12 - 4) - 4$
$16 \times 8 - 4$
$128 - 4$
124

10) $7 \times (4 \times 10 + 4^2) - 3$
$7 \times (4 \times 10 + 16) - 3$
$7 \times (40 + 16) - 3$
$7 \times 56 - 3$
$392 - 3$
389

Day 75

1) $(21 + 3) \times (14 - 4) - 4^2$

    $(21 + 3) \times (14 - 4) - 16$

    24   x   10   - 16

        240   - 16

            224

2) $6 \times (13 \times 9 + 8^2) - 6$

    $6 \times (13 \times 9 + 64) - 6$

    $6 \times (117 + 64) - 6$

    6 x   181   - 6

    1086   - 6

        1080

3) $(11 - 2) \times (10 - 6) + 2^2$

    $(11 - 2) \times (10 - 6) + 4$

    9   x   4   + 4

      36   + 4

        40

4) $3 \times (6 \times 6 + 8^2) - 5$

    $3 \times (6 \times 6 + 64) - 5$

    $3 \times (36 + 64) - 5$

    3 x   100   - 5

    300   - 5

        295

5) $(13 - 2)^2 + (9 + 10 + 5)$

    $(11)^2 + (9 + 15)$

    121   +   24

        145

6) $(14 + 61 - 5^2) + (4 - 2)$

    $(14 + 61 - 25) + (4 - 2)$

    (75 - 25) +   2

      50   +   2

        52

7) $(3 + 4)^2 + (16 + 20 + 5)$

    $(7)^2 + (16 + 25)$

    49   +   41

        90

8) $(9 + 18 - 3) - 12 - 2^2$

    $(9 + 18 - 3) - 12 - 4$

    (27 - 3) - 12 - 4

      24   - 12 - 4

        12   - 4

        8

9) $(10 + 18 - 4) - 2 + 3^2$

    $(10 + 18 - 4) - 2 + 9$

    (28 - 4) - 2 + 9

      24   - 2 + 9

        22   + 9

        31

10) $(9 + 35 - 2^2) + (2 + 6)$

    $(9 + 35 - 4) + (2 + 6)$

    (44 - 4) +   8

      40   +   8

        48

Day 76

1) $(12 + 3) \times (11 - 4) - 5^2$
$(12 + 3) \times (11 - 4) - 25$
$15 \quad \times \quad 7 \quad - 25$
$105 \quad\quad - 25$
80

2) $(9 - 4)^2 + (7 + 16 + 2)$
$(\quad 5 \quad)^2 + (7 + \quad 18 \quad)$
$25 \quad + \quad 25$
50

3) $(11 - 3) \times (11 + 6) + 8^2$
$(11 - 3) \times (11 + 6) + 64$
$8 \quad \times \quad 17 \quad + 64$
$136 \quad\quad + 64$
200

4) $(10 - 4)^2 + (9 + 18 + 9)$
$(\quad 6 \quad)^2 + (9 + \quad 27 \quad)$
$36 \quad + \quad 36$
72

5) $8 \times (11 \times 3 + 3^2) + 8$
$8 \times (11 \times 3 + 9) + 8$
$8 \times (33 \quad + 9) + 8$
$8 \times \quad 42 \quad + 8$
$336 \quad\quad + 8$
344

6) $(15 + 20 - 5) - 2 - 2^2$
$(15 + 20 - 5) - 2 - 4$
$(\quad 35 \quad - 5) - 2 - 4$
$30 \quad - 2 - 4$
$28 \quad - 4$
24

7) $(11 + 26 - 3^2) + (3 + 4)$
$(11 + 26 - 9) + (3 + 4)$
$(\quad 37 \quad - 9) + \quad 7$
$28 \quad + \quad 7$
35

8) $6 \times (13 \times 5 - 6^2) - 10$
$6 \times (13 \times 5 - 36) - 10$
$6 \times (\quad 65 \quad - 36) - 10$
$6 \times \quad 29 \quad - 10$
$174 \quad\quad - 10$
164

9) $(9 + 48 - 5^2) + (3 + 5)$
$(9 + 48 - 25) + (3 + 5)$
$(\quad 57 \quad - 25) + \quad 8$
$32 \quad + \quad 8$
40

10) $(10 + 23 - 5) - 7 - 3^2$
$(10 + 23 - 5) - 7 - 9$
$(\quad 33 \quad - 5) - 7 - 9$
$28 \quad - 7 - 9$
$21 \quad - 9$
12

Day 77

1) $(14 - 4) \times (10 + 2) + 2^2$

$(14 - 4) \times (10 + 2) + 4$

$10 \quad \times \quad 12 \quad + 4$

$120 \qquad + 4$

124

2) $(10 + 55 - 5) - 6 + 6^2$

$(10 + 55 - 5) - 6 + 36$

$(\quad 65 \quad - 5) - 6 + 36$

$60 \qquad - 6 + 36$

$54 \quad + 36$

90

3) $(8 + 20 - 2^2) + (1 + 3)$

$(8 + 20 - 4 \ ) + (1 + 3)$

$(\quad 28 \quad - 4) + \quad 4$

$24 \qquad + \quad 4$

28

4) $(12 - 3)^2 + (12 + 24 + 12)$

$(\quad 9 \quad)^2 + (12 + \quad 36 \quad)$

$81 \quad + \qquad 48$

129

5) $(9 + 60 - 3^2) + (35 - 5)$

$(9 + 60 - 9 \ ) + (35 - 5)$

$(\quad 69 \quad - 9) + \quad 30$

$60 \qquad + \quad 30$

90

6) $(11 - 6) \times (13 - 3) + 6^2$

$(11 - 6) \times (13 - 3) + 36$

$5 \quad \times \quad 10 \quad + 36$

$50 \qquad + 36$

86

7) $8 \times (12 \times 10 + 8^2) - 8$

$8 \times (12 \times 10 + 64) - 8$

$8 \times (120 \quad + 64) - 8$

$8 \times \quad 184 \qquad - 8$

$1472 \qquad - 8$

1464

8) $4 \times (3 \times 9 - 6^2) - 4$

$4 \times (3 \times 9 - 36) - 4$

$4 \times (27 \quad - 36) - 4$

$4 \times \quad -9 \qquad - 4$

$-36 \qquad - 4$

-40

9) $(6 + 4)^2 + (13 + 15 - 3)$

$(\quad 10 \quad)^2 + (13 + \quad 12 \quad)$

$100 \quad + \qquad 25$

125

10) $(12 + 30 - 6) - 12 + 6^2$

$(12 + 30 - 6) - 12 + 36$

$(\quad 42 \quad - 6) - 12 + 36$

$36 \qquad - 12 + 36$

$24 \quad + 36$

60

Day 78

1) $8 \times (2 \times 6 + 7^2) - 7$
    $8 \times (2 \times 6 + 49) - 7$
    $8 \times (12 \quad + 49) - 7$
    $8 \times \quad 61 \qquad - 7$
      $488 \qquad\qquad - 7$
               481

2) $(11 + 39 - 2) - 24 + 4^2$
    $(11 + 39 - 2) - 24 + 16$
    $(\quad 50 \quad - 2) - 24 + 16$
       $48 \qquad - 24 + 16$
          $24 \quad + 16$
              40

3) $(20 - 5) \times (10 + 3) - 5^2$
    $(20 - 5) \times (10 + 3) - 25$
      $15 \quad \times \quad 13 \quad - 25$
       $195 \qquad\quad - 25$
              170

4) $(3 + 4)^2 + (11 + 8 + 4)$
    $(\quad 7 \quad)^2 + (11 + \quad 12 \quad)$
      $49 \quad + \qquad 23$
             72

5) $(12 + 54 - 6^2) + (8 - 5)$
    $(12 + 54 - 36) + (8 - 5)$
    $(\quad 66 \quad - 36) + \qquad 3$
      $30 \qquad + \quad 3$
            33

6) $(18 - 8) \times (9 + 6) - 4^2$
    $(18 - 8) \times (9 + 6) - 16$
      $10 \quad \times \quad 15 \quad - 16$
        $150 \qquad - 16$
              134

7) $(7 + 4)^2 + (5 + 24 - 6)$
    $(\quad 11 \quad)^2 + (5 + \quad 18 \quad)$
      $121 \quad + \qquad 23$
              144

8) $(12 + 34 - 6) - 8 - 5^2$
    $(12 + 34 - 6) - 8 - 25$
    $(\quad 46 \quad - 6) - 8 - 25$
       $40 \qquad - 8 - 25$
         $32 \quad - 25$
              7

9) $(10 + 30 - 4^2) + (-3 + 5)$
    $(10 + 30 - 16) + (-3 + 5)$
    $(\quad 40 \quad - 16) + \quad 2$
       $24 \qquad + \quad 2$
              26

10) $4 \times (7 \times 8 + 6^2) - 7$
    $4 \times (7 \times 8 + 36) - 7$
    $4 \times (56 \quad + 36) - 7$
    $4 \times \quad 92 \qquad 7$
      $368 \qquad\qquad - 7$
               361

Day 79

1) $3 \times (3 \times 10 + 4^2) - 3$
   $3 \times (3 \times 10 + 16) - 3$
   $3 \times (30 + 16) - 3$
   $3 \times 46 - 3$
   $138 - 3$
   135

2) $(15 + 6) \times (10 - 5) - 3^2$
   $(15 + 6) \times (10 - 5) - 9$
   $21 \times 5 - 9$
   $105 - 9$
   96

3) $(12 + 27 - 3^2) + (11 + 4)$
   $(12 + 27 - 9) + (11 + 4)$
   $(39 - 9) + 15$
   $30 + 15$
   45

4) $(9 - 2)^2 + (6 + 10 + 5)$
   $(7)^2 + (6 + 15)$
   $49 + 21$
   70

5) $7 \times (9 \times 8 - 4^2) - 10$
   $7 \times (9 \times 8 - 16) - 10$
   $7 \times (72 - 16) - 10$
   $7 \times 56 - 10$
   $392 - 10$
   382

6) $(12 + 21 - 3) - 6 - 5^2$
   $(12 + 21 - 3) - 6 - 25$
   $(33 - 3) - 6 - 25$
   $30 - 6 - 25$
   $24 - 25$
   -1

7) $(9 + 25 - 2^2) + (8 - 2)$
   $(9 + 25 - 4) + (8 - 2)$
   $(34 - 4) + 6$
   $30 + 6$
   36

8) $(9 + 3)^2 + (10 + 14 - 7)$
   $(12)^2 + (10 + 7)$
   $144 + 17$
   161

9) $(21 - 8) \times (14 + 3) - 4^2$
   $(21 - 8) \times (14 + 3) - 16$
   $13 \times 17 - 16$
   $221 - 16$
   205

10) $(13 + 16 - 5) - 3 + 2^2$
   $(13 + 16 - 5) - 3 + 4$
   $(29 - 5) - 3 + 4$
   $24 - 3 + 4$
   $21 + 4$
   25

Day 80

1) $9 \times (13 \times 8 + 5^2) + 2$
   $9 \times (13 \times 8 + 25) + 2$
   $9 \times (104 \qquad + 25) + 2$
   $9 \times \qquad 129 \qquad + 2$
   $1161 \qquad\qquad + 2$
   $\qquad\qquad\qquad 1163$

2) $(8 + 27 - 5) - 6 - 6^2$
   $(8 + 27 - 5) - 6 - 36$
   $(\quad 35 \quad - 5) - 6 - 36$
   $\qquad 30 \qquad - 6 - 36$
   $\qquad\qquad 24 \quad - 36$
   $\qquad\qquad\qquad -12$

3) $(12 + 18 - 2) - 7 - 3^2$
   $(12 + 18 - 2) - 7 - 9$
   $(\quad 30 \quad - 2) - 7 - 9$
   $\qquad 28 \qquad - 7 - 9$
   $\qquad\qquad 21 \quad - 9$
   $\qquad\qquad\qquad 12$

4) $(14 - 2) \times (13 + 2) - 3^2$
   $(14 - 2) \times (13 + 2) - 9$
   $\quad 12 \quad \times \quad 15 \quad - 9$
   $\qquad 180 \qquad\quad - 9$
   $\qquad\qquad\qquad 171$

5) $(10 - 3)^2 + (11 + 18 - 3)$
   $(\quad 7 \quad)^2 + (11 + \quad 15 \quad)$
   $\qquad 49 \quad + \qquad 26$
   $\qquad\qquad\qquad 76$

6) $(20 - 5) \times (11 + 6) - 8^2$
   $(20 - 5) \times (11 + 6) - 64$
   $\quad 15 \quad \times \quad 17 \quad - 64$
   $\qquad 255 \qquad\quad - 64$
   $\qquad\qquad\qquad 191$

7) $(8 + 4)^2 + (6 + 14 + 7)$
   $(\quad 12 \quad)^2 + (6 + \quad 21 \quad)$
   $\qquad 144 \quad + \qquad 27$
   $\qquad\qquad\qquad 171$

8) $3 \times (9 \times 7 + 7^2) + 10$
   $3 \times (9 \times 7 + 49) + 10$
   $3 \times (\quad 63 \qquad + 49) + 10$
   $3 \times \qquad 112 \qquad + 10$
   $\qquad 336 \qquad\qquad + 10$
   $\qquad\qquad\qquad 346$

9) $(10 + 24 - 2^2) + (4 - 2)$
   $(10 + 24 - 4) + (4 - 2)$
   $(\quad 34 \quad - 4) + \quad 2$
   $\qquad 30 \qquad + \quad 2$
   $\qquad\qquad\qquad 32$

10) $(12 + 54 - 6^2) + (7 - 5)$
   $(12 + 54 - 36) + (7 - 5)$
   $(\quad 66 \quad - 36) + \quad 2$
   $\qquad 30 \qquad + \quad 2$
   $\qquad\qquad\qquad 32$

Day 81

1) (5 +(15 + 3 - 4)) + 5
   (5 +(18   - 4)) + 5
   (5 +   14   ) + 5
       19   + 5
            24

2) ((12 - 5) + 6) + 5 + 3
   (7   + 6) + 5 + 3
      13   + 5 + 3
             21

3) (10 - 5)+ ((10 - 4) x 2)
     5   +(6   x 2)
     5   +   12
          17

4) ((18 + 6) - (14 - 2)) + 7
   (24   -   12   ) + 7
      12   + 7
         19

5) ((10 - 3) + 3) - 2 - 3
   (7   + 3) - 2 - 3
      10   - 2 - 3
         5

6) 16 +(8 +(18 - 2)) - 3
  16 +(8 +   16   ) - 3
  16 +   24   - 3
          37

7) ((15 - 5) +(14 - 2)) x 5
  (10   +   12   ) x 5
      22   x 5
         110

8) (13 +(20 + 4 + 6)) - 4
  (13 +(24   + 6)) - 4
  (13 +   30   ) - 4
      43   - 4
        39

9) 19 +(7 x (14 + 6)) + 4
  19 +(7 x   20   ) + 4
  19 +   140   + 4
        163

10) (12 - 2)+ ((11 - 4) + 2)
    10   +(7   + 2)
    10   +   9
       19

Day 82

1) ((9 + 5) - (24 - 4)) x 7
(14 - 20) x 7
-6 x 7
-42

2) (2 +(10 + 2 - 5)) - 2
(2 +(12 - 5)) - 2
(2 + 7) - 2
9 - 2
7

3) (16 - 2)+ ((15 + 3) x 5)
14 +(18 x 5)
14 + 90
104

4) ((12 - 2) - (15 - 5)) x 3
(10 - 10) x 3
0 x 3
0

5) ((11 - 4) + 4) - 4 + 3
(7 + 4) - 4 + 3
11 - 4 + 3
10

6) ((12 - 7) x 6) + 9 - 10
(5 x 6) + 9 - 10
30 + 9 - 10
29

7) 9 +(3 + (12 + 6)) + 7
9 +(3 + 18) + 7
9 + 21 + 7
37

8) (12 - 3) + ((14 - 4) x 3)
9 +(10 x 3)
9 + 30
39

9) 4 +(4 x (10 + 4)) - 8
4 +(4 x 14) - 8
4 + 56 - 8
52

10) (8 +(10 + 5 + 8)) - 9
(8 +(15 + 8)) - 9
(8 + 23) - 9
31 9

Day 83

1) 9 + (4 x (13 - 7)) + 3
     9 + (4 x   6   ) + 3
     9 +   24   + 3
                        36

2) ((11 - 2) + (20 - 4)) x 5
    (9   +   16   ) x 5
              25   x 5
                        125

3) (24 - 6) + ((17 - 2) x 5)
        18   + (15   x 5)
        18   +   75
                        93

4) ((10 - 3) + 6) + 12 + 10
     (7   + 6) + 12 + 10
             13   + 12 + 10
                        35

5) (10 + (24 + 2 - 9)) + 6
     (10 + (26   - 9)) + 6
     (10 +   17   ) + 6
             27   + 6
                        33

6) 19 + (6 + (17 + 4)) - 4
     19 + (6 +   21   ) - 4
     19 +   27   - 4
                        42

7) ((12 - 5) x 5) + 4 - 10
    (7   x 5) + 4 - 10
            35   + 4 - 10
                        29

8) ((10 - 5) + (12 - 3)) x 2
    (5   +   9   ) x 2
              14   x 2
                        28

9) (10 + (14 + 7 - 9)) + 5
     (10 + (21   - 9)) + 5
     (10 +   12   ) + 5
             22   + 5
                        27

10) (10 - 5) + ((12 + 5) x 2)
          5   + (17   x 2)
          5   +   34
                        39

Day 84

1) (2 + (20 + 2 + 2)) - 6
(2 + (22   + 2)) - 6
(2 +   24   ) - 6
        26   - 6
                    20

2) (10 - 2) + ((17 - 7) x 5)
      8   + (10   x 5)
      8   +   50
                  58

3) ((17 - 6) + 7) + 4 - 4
(11   + 7) + 4 - 4
      18   + 4 - 4
                  18

4) (10 - 2) + ((10 + 3) + 4)
      8   + (13   + 4)
      8   +   17
                  25

5)   2 + (8 + (14 - 6)) + 7
      2 + (8 +   8   ) + 7
      2 +   16   + 7
                  25

6) (11 + (12 + 4 + 3)) - 3
(11 + (16   + 3)) - 3
(11 +   19   ) - 3
        30   - 3
                    27

7) ((9 + 5) - (15 - 5)) + 7
(14   -   10   ) + 7
            4   + 7
                    11

8) ((18 + 2) - (20 - 10)) + 7
(20   -   10   ) + 7
            10   + 7
                    17

9)   17 + (6 x (17 - 3)) - 3
17 + (6 x   14   ) - 3
17 +   84   - 3
                    98

10) ((16 + 2) x 3) - 6 - 9
(18   x 3) - 6 - 9
            54   - 6 - 9
                    39

Day 85

1) ((12 - 4) x 5) + 10 - 9
(8   x 5) + 10 - 9
     40   + 10 - 9
           41

2) (8 + (12 + 3 + 6)) - 3
(8 + (15   + 6)) - 3
(8 +   21   ) - 3
    29   - 3
         26

3) (16 - 4) + ((11 + 7) + 4)
   12   + (18   + 4)
   12   +   22
        34

4) (18 - 9) + ((11 - 7) x 5)
    9   + (4   x 5)
    9   +   20
        29

5) ((16 + 3) + (8 - 4)) x 3
(19   +   4   ) x 3
     23   x 3
         69

6) 9 + (2 + (9 - 3)) + 10
9 + (2 +   6   ) + 10
9 +   8   + 10
        27

7) ((17 + 7) - (24 - 6)) + 4
(24   -   18   ) + 4
      6   + 4
        10

8) ((18 - 4) + 4) + 5 - 3
(14   + 4) + 5 - 3
     18   + 5 - 3
        20

9) 14 + (4 + (15 - 8)) + 3
14 + (4 +   7   ) + 3
14 +   11   + 3
        28

10) (9 + (12 + 3 - 5)) - 2
(9 + (15   - 5)) - 2
(9 +   10   ) - 2
     19   - 2
        17

Day 86

1) 15 + (6 + (10 + 4)) - 9
   15 + (6 +   14   ) - 9
   15 +   20   - 9
                      26

2) (12 - 3) + ((9 + 3) x 5)
     9   + (12   x 5)
     9   +   60
              69

3) ((10 + 4) - (18 - 6)) x 7
   (14   -   12   ) x 7
         2   x 7
               14

4) ((10 - 4) + (24 - 8)) + 2
   (6   +   16   ) + 2
       22   + 2
             24

5) (4 + (18 + 6 - 5)) - 5
   (4 + (24   - 5)) - 5
   (4 +   19   ) - 5
     23   5

6) ((18 - 4) x 6) + 4 - 8
   (14   x 6) + 4 - 8
        84   + 4 - 8
             80

7) (7 + (12 + 2 - 7)) + 7
   (7 + (14   - 7)) + 7
   (7 +   7   ) + 7
      14   + 7
            21

8) (16 - 8) + ((18 - 4) x 2)
     8   + (14   x 2)
     8   +   28
          36

9) ((17 + 2) x 4) - 8 - 7
   (19   x 4) - 8 - 7
       76   - 8 - 7
             61

10) 12 + (9 x (13 + 6)) - 3
    12 + (9 x   19   ) - 3
    12 +   171   - 3
             180

Day 87

1) (6 +(18 + 6 - 5)) + 5
(6 +(24 - 5)) + 5
(6 + 19) + 5
25 + 5
30

2) ((14 +5) + 5) - 10 + 3
(19 + 5) - 10 + 3
24 - 10 + 3
17

3) ((14 - 2) - (20 - 10)) x 2
(12 - 10) x 2
2 x 2
4

4) ((10 - 5) x 4) + 3 + 8
(5 x 4) + 3 + 8
20 + 3 + 8
31

5) (16 - 2) + ((14 - 7) x 6)
14 + (7 x 6)
14 + 42
56

6) ((18 - 3) - (8 - 2)) + 6
(15 - 6) + 6
9 + 6
15

7) 13 +(10 x (14 - 3)) +10
13 +(10 x 11) +10
13 + 110 +10
133

8) (7 +(15 + 3 - 2)) - 2
(7 +(18 - 2)) - 2
(7 + 16) - 2
23 - 2
21

9) (15 - 3) + ((15 - 7) x 6)
12 + (8 x 6)
12 + 48
60

10) 10 +(10 + (16 - 7)) - 6
10 +(10 + 9) - 6
10 + 19 - 6
23

Day 88

1) 19 + (10 + (17 + 4)) + 2
    19 + (10 +   21   ) + 2
    19 +   31   + 2
                   52

6) ((16 + 7) - (10 - 2)) x 3
    (23   -   8) x 3
              15   x 3
                   45

2) (12 - 4) + ((14 - 4) x 5)
     8   + (10   x 5)
     8   +   50
               58

7) 3 + (5 x (12 + 2)) + 6
    3 + (5 x   14   ) + 6
    3 +   70   + 6
                79

3) ((18 - 5) + 7) + 12 - 4
    (13   + 7) + 12 - 4
        20   + 12 - 4
             28

8) ((11 - 6) - (15 - 3)) + 2
    (5   -   12   ) + 2
       -7   + 2
             -5

4) (20 - 4) + ((13 - 2) + 4)
    16   + (11   + 4)
    16   +   15
           31

9) (10 + (18 + 6 - 2)) + 7
    (10 + (24 - 2)) + 7
    (10 +   22   ) + 7
       32   + 7
           39

5) (2 + (24 + 8 + 6)) - 8
    (2 + (32   + 6)) - 8
    (2 +   38   ) - 8
      40   - 8

10) ((13 - 7) x 5) - 12 + 3
    (6   x 5) - 12 + 3
       30   - 12 + 3
           21

Day 89

1) (6 +(16 + 2 - 8)) - 8
   (6 +(18   - 8)) - 8
   (6 +   10   ) - 8
          16   - 8
                     8

2) (2 +(15 + 5 - 3)) - 2
   (2 +(20   - 3)) - 2
   (2 +   17   ) - 2
         19   - 2
                   17

3) 15 +(2 x (15 + 3)) - 4
   15 +(2 x   18) - 4
   15 +   36   - 4
                   47

4) (16 - 8)+((10 + 3) x 6)
    8   +(13   x 6)
    8   +   78
              86

5) 13 +(3 x (10 - 2)) + 7
   13 +(3 x   8) + 7
   13 +   24   + 7
              44

6) ((11 - 8) + 4) + 8 + 7
   (3   + 4) + 8 + 7
        7   + 8 + 7
              22

7) ((10 + 4) +(8 - 2)) x 5
   (14 +   6) x 5
        20   x 5
             100

8) (18 - 3)+((14 + 2) + 6)
    15   +(16 + 6)
    15   +   22
            37

9) ((9 +6) x 5) - 11 +10
   (15 x 5) - 11 +10
      75   - 11 +10
           74

10) ((13 + 7) - (18 - 2)) + 2
   (20 - 16) + 2
       4   + 2
          6

Day 90

1) (2 +(8 + 2 - 5)) + 7
   (2 +(10 - 5)) + 7
   (2 +   5   ) + 7
        7   + 7
                14

2) (8 - 2)+((13 - 6) x 3)
     6 +(7   x 3)
     6 +   21
           27

3) 5 +(8 x (17 + 2)) - 10
   5 +(8 x   19) - 10
   5 +   152   - 10
             147

4) ((13 - 3) - (24 - 2)) + 7
   (10 -   22) + 7
              + 7
             -5

5) ((15 + 6) +(8 - 2)) x 4
   (21 +   6) x 4
        27   x 4
           108

6) ((13 +6) x 3) + 4 - 4
   (19 x 3) + 4 - 4
       57   + 4 - 4
             57

7) 2 +(6 x (10 - 8)) + 9
   2 +(6 x   2) + 9
   2 +   12   + 9
             23

8) (15 - 3) + ((15 + 7) x 5)
    12 +(22   x 5)
    12 +   110
          122

9) ((12 +5) + 6) + 9 - 7
   (17 + 6) + 9 - 7
       23   + 9 - 7
            25

10) (11 +(10 + 2 + 2)) + 5
   (11 +(12 + 2)) + 5
   (11 +   14   ) + 5
       25   + 5
             30

Day 91

1) $(16 - 2)^2 + ((18 + 3) \times 2^2)$
$(\quad 14 \quad)^2 + (\quad 21 \quad \times 2^2)$
$\quad 196 \quad + (\quad 21 \quad \times 4)$
$\quad 196 \quad + \quad\quad 84$
$\quad\quad\quad\quad\quad 280$

2) $((17 + 7) + (12 - 4)^2) \times 6^2$
$(\quad 24 \quad + (\quad 8 \quad)^2) \times 6^2$
$(\quad 24 \quad + \quad 64 \quad) \times 6^2$
$\quad\quad\quad 88 \quad\quad\quad \times 6^2$
$\quad\quad\quad 88 \quad\quad\quad \times 36$
$\quad\quad\quad\quad\quad\quad 3168$

3) $(10 - 2)^2 + ((13 - 2) \times 5^2)$
$(\quad 8 \quad)^2 + (\quad 11 \quad \times 5^2)$
$\quad 64 \quad + (\quad 11 \quad \times 25)$
$\quad 64 \quad + \quad\quad 275$
$\quad\quad\quad\quad 339$

4) $(4^2 + (16 - 2 + 5^2)) + 5^2$
$(4^2 + (16 - 2 + 25)) + 5^2$
$(4^2 + (\quad 14 \quad + 25)) + 5^2$
$(16 + \quad\quad 39 \quad\quad) + 25$
$\quad\quad 55 \quad\quad\quad + 25$
$\quad\quad\quad\quad\quad 80$

5) $6 + (8 \times (10 - 2)^2) - 7$
$6 + (8 \times \quad 8^2 \quad) - 7$
$6 + (8 \times \quad 64 \quad) - 7$
$6 + \quad 512 \quad\quad\quad - 7$
$\quad\quad\quad\quad\quad 511$

6) $(5^2 + (12 - 3 + 2^2)) + 2^2$
$(5^2 + (12 - 3 + 4)) + 2^2$
$(5^2 + (\quad 9 \quad + 4)) + 2^2$
$(25 + \quad\quad 13 \quad\quad) + 4$
$\quad\quad 38 \quad\quad\quad + 4$
$\quad\quad\quad\quad\quad 42$

7) $((11 - 4)^2 + 2) - 6 + 7^2$
$(\quad 7^2 \quad + 2) - 6 + 49$
$(\quad 49 \quad + 2) - 6 + 49$
$\quad\quad 51 \quad\quad - 6 + 49$
$\quad\quad\quad\quad\quad 94$

8) $((17 + 2) + (15 - 5)^2) + 2^2$
$(\quad 19 \quad + (\quad 10 \quad)^2) + 2^2$
$(\quad 19 \quad + \quad 100 \quad) + 2^2$
$\quad\quad\quad 119 \quad\quad\quad + 2^2$
$\quad\quad\quad 119 \quad\quad\quad + 4$
$\quad\quad\quad\quad\quad\quad 123$

9) $3 + (2 + (10 - 6)^2) + 9$
$3 + (2 + \quad 4^2 \quad) + 9$
$3 + (2 + \quad 16 \quad) + 9$
$3 + \quad\quad 18 \quad\quad + 9$
$\quad\quad\quad\quad\quad 30$

10) $((3 + 2)^2 \times 4) - 12 - 3^2$
$(\quad 5^2 \quad \times 4) - 12 - 9$
$(\quad 25 \quad \times 4) - 12 - 9$
$\quad\quad 100 \quad\quad - 12 - 9$
$\quad\quad\quad\quad\quad 79$

Day 92

1) $(18 - 3)^2 + ((10 - 6) + 4^2)$
    $(\quad 15 \quad)^2 + (\quad 4 \quad + 4^2)$
    $225 \quad + (\quad 4 \quad + 16)$
    $225 \quad + \quad 20$
            245

2) $((11 + 6) + (18 - 6)^2) \times 6^2$
    $(\quad 17 \quad + (\quad 12 \quad)^2) \times 6^2$
    $(\quad 17 \quad + \quad 144 \quad) \times 6^2$
         $161 \quad\quad\quad \times 6^2$
         $161 \quad\quad\quad \times 36$
           5796

3) $(12 - 6)^2 + ((16 + 5) \times 2^2)$
    $(\quad 6 \quad)^2 + (\quad 21 \quad \times 2^2)$
      $36 \quad + (\quad 21 \quad \times 4)$
      $36 \quad + \quad\quad 84$
          120

4) $2 + (2 \times (6 + 5)^2) - 8$
    $2 + (2 \times \quad 11^2 \quad) - 8$
    $2 + (2 \times \quad 121 \quad) - 8$
    $2 + \quad 242 \quad\quad\quad - 8$
          236

5) $8 + (2 \times (9 - 6)^2) - 2$
    $8 + (2 \times \quad 3^2 \quad) - 2$
    $8 + (2 \times \quad 9 \quad) - 2$
    $8 + \quad 18 \quad\quad\quad 2$
         24

6) $((6 + 2)^2 + 7) - 9 - 2^2$
    $(\quad 8^2 \quad + 7) - 9 - 4$
    $(\quad 64 \quad + 7) - 9 - 4$
       $71 \quad\quad - 9 - 4$
         58

7) $(7^2 + (20 - 10 + 5^2)) - 5^2$
    $(7^2 + (20 - 10 + 25)) - 5^2$
    $(7^2 + (\quad 10 \quad + 25)) - 5^2$
    $(49 + \quad 35 \quad) - 25$
       $84 \quad\quad - 25$
         59

8) $(4^2 + (10 - 2 + 4^2)) - 5^2$
    $(4^2 + (10 - 2 + 16)) - 5^2$
    $(4^2 + (\quad 8 \quad + 16)) - 5^2$
    $(16 + \quad 24 \quad) - 25$
       $40 \quad\quad - 25$
         15

9) $((9 - 5)^2 \times 4) - 10 + 3^2$
    $(\quad 4^2 \quad \times 4) - 10 + 9$
    $(\quad 16 \quad \times 4) - 10 + 9$
       $64 \quad\quad - 10 + 9$
         63

10) $((16 - 3) + (8 - 4)^2) + 5^2$
    $(\quad 13 \quad + (\quad 4 \quad)^2) + 5^2$
    $(\quad 13 \quad + \quad 16 \quad) + 5^2$
        $29 \quad\quad\quad + 5^2$
        $29 \quad\quad\quad + 25$
           54

Day 93

1) $(20 - 5)^2 + ((12 + 3) + 3^2)$
    (15 $)^2 + ($ 15 $+ 3^2)$
    225 + (15 + 9)
    225 + 24
          249

2) $((3 + 5)^2 \times 6) - 12 + 4^2$
    (8^2 $\times 6) - 12 + 16$
    (64 $\times 6) - 12 + 16$
      384 - 12 + 16
          388

3) $(3^2 + (16 - 2 + 4^2)) - 4^2$
    $(3^2 + (16 - 2 + 16)) - 4^2$
    $(3^2 + (14 + 16)) - 4^2$
    (9 + 30) - 16
      39 - 16
          23

4) $6 + (2 \times (4 + 4)^2) - 5$
    $6 + (2 \times 8^2) - 5$
    $6 + (2 \times 64) - 5$
    6 + 128 - 5
          129

5) $(8 - 4)^2 + ((11 - 5) \times 3^2)$
    (4 $)^2 + ($ 6 $\times 3^2)$
    16 + (6 $\times 9$)
    16 + 54
          70

6) $(5^2 + (16 - 8 + 5^2)) - 2^2$
    $(5^2 + (16 - 8 + 25)) - 2^2$
    $(5^2 + (8 + 25)) - 2^2$
    (25 + 33) - 4
      58 - 4
          54

7) $13 + (5 \times (9 - 4)^2) + 3$
    $13 + (5 \times 5^2) + 3$
    $13 + (5 \times 25) + 3$
    13 + 125 + 3
          141

8) $((10 - 6)^2 \times 6) + 10 - 4^2$
    (4^2 $\times 6) + 10 - 16$
    (16 $\times 6) + 10 - 16$
      96 + 10 - 16
          90

9) $((15 + 7) + (16 - 8)^2) + 4^2$
    (22 $+ ($ 8 $)^2) + 4^2$
    (22 + 64) $+ 4^2$
      86 $+ 4^2$
      86 + 16
          102

10) $((11 - 7) + (10 - 5)^2) \times 2^2$
    (4 $+ ($ 5 $)^2) \times 2^2$
    (4 + 25) $\times 2^2$
      29 $\times 2^2$
      29 $\times 4$
          116

Day 94

1) $((10 - 6)^2 \times 6) - 8 + 4^2$
    $(\quad 4^2 \quad \times 6) - 8 + 16$
    $(\quad 16 \quad \times 6) - 8 + 16$
         $96 \qquad - 8 + 16$
                    104

2) $(15 - 3)^2 + ((12 + 6) \times 6^2)$
    $(\quad 12 \quad)^2 + (\quad 18 \quad \times 6^2)$
    $144 \quad + (\quad 18 \quad \times 36)$
    $144 \quad + \qquad 648$
                792

3) $(15 - 5)^2 + ((14 - 5) \times 6^2)$
    $(\quad 10 \quad)^2 + (\quad 9 \quad \times 6^2)$
    $100 \quad + (\quad 9 \quad \times 36)$
    $100 \quad + \qquad 324$
                424

4) $((13 - 2) + (18 - 9)^2) \times 7^2$
    $(\quad 11 \quad + (\quad 9 \quad)^2) \times 7^2$
    $(\quad 11 \quad + \quad 81 \quad) \times 7^2$
         $92 \qquad\qquad \times 7^2$
         $92 \qquad\qquad \times 49$
                4508

5) $(6^2 + (14 - 2 + 4^2)) + 2^2$
    $(6^2 + (14 - 2 + 16)) + 2^2$
    $(6^2 + (\quad 12 \quad + 16)) + 2^2$
    $(36 + \qquad 28 \qquad) + 4$
        $64 \qquad\qquad + 4$
                68

6) $((9 - 2) + (16 - 4)^2) + 6^2$
    $(\quad 7 \quad + (\quad 12 \quad)^2) + 6^2$
    $(\quad 7 \quad + \quad 144 \quad) + 6^2$
        $151 \qquad\qquad + 6^2$
        $151 \qquad\qquad + 36$
                187

7) $4 + (6 \times (11 - 6)^2) - 7$
    $4 + (6 \times \quad 5^2 \quad) - 7$
    $4 + (6 \times \quad 25 \quad) - 7$
    $4 + \qquad 150 \qquad - 7$
                147

8) $((4 + 4)^2 + 3) - 5 - 2^2$
    $(\quad 8^2 \quad + 3) - 5 - 4$
    $(\quad 64 \quad + 3) - 5 - 4$
        $67 \qquad - 5 - 4$
                58

9) $2 + (2 \times (5 + 6)^2) - 6$
    $2 + (2 \times \quad 11^2 \quad) - 6$
    $2 + (2 \times \quad 121 \quad) - 6$
    $2 + \quad 242 \qquad - 6$
                238

10) $(5^2 + (18 - 3 + 2^2)) + 2^2$
    $(5^2 + (18 - 3 + 4)) + 2^2$
    $(5^2 + (\quad 15 \quad + 4)) + 2^2$
    $(25 + \qquad 19 \qquad) + 4$
        $44 \qquad\qquad + 4$
                48

Day 95

1) $(8 - 2)^2 + ((15 - 4) + 3^2)$
$(\quad 6\quad)^2 + (\quad 11\quad + 3^2)$
$\quad 36\quad + (\quad 11\quad + 9)$
$\quad 36\quad +\quad\quad 20$
$\quad\quad\quad\quad 56$

2) $16 + (9 + (3 + 2)^2) + 8$
$16 + (9 +\quad 5^2\quad) + 8$
$16 + (9 +\quad 25\quad) + 8$
$16 +\quad 34\quad\quad + 8$
$\quad\quad\quad\quad 58$

3) $(7^2 + (10 - 2 + 4^2)) - 2^2$
$(7^2 + (10 - 2 + 16)) - 2^2$
$(7^2 + (\quad 8\quad + 16)) - 2^2$
$(49 +\quad 24\quad) - 4$
$\quad\quad 73\quad\quad - 4$
$\quad\quad\quad\quad 69$

4) $(12 - 2)^2 + ((12 - 5) \times 6^2)$
$(\quad 10\quad)^2 + (\quad 7\quad \times 6^2)$
$\quad 100\quad + (\quad 7\quad \times 36)$
$\quad 100\quad +\quad\quad 252$
$\quad\quad\quad\quad 352$

5) $13 + (3 \times (3 + 4)^2) + 4$
$13 + (3 \times\quad 7^2\quad) + 4$
$13 + (3 \times\quad 49\quad) + 4$
$13 +\quad 147\quad\quad + 4$
$\quad\quad\quad\quad 164$

6) $((11 - 4)^2 \times 5) - 8 + 2^2$
$(\quad 7^2\quad \times 5) - 8 + 4$
$(\quad 49\quad \times 5) - 8 + 4$
$\quad 245\quad\quad - 8 + 4$
$\quad\quad\quad\quad 241$

7) $((6 + 3)^2 \times 5) + 4 - 4^2$
$(\quad 9^2\quad \times 5) + 4 - 16$
$(\quad 81\quad \times 5) + 4 - 16$
$\quad\quad 405\quad + 4 - 16$
$\quad\quad\quad\quad 393$

8) $(3^2 + (14 - 7 + 3^2)) - 5^2$
$(3^2 + (14 - 7 + 9)) - 5^2$
$(3^2 + (\quad 7\quad + 9)) - 5^2$
$(9 +\quad\quad 16\quad) - 25$
$\quad\quad 25\quad\quad - 25$
$\quad\quad\quad\quad 0$

9) $((12 + 7) + (10 - 5)^2) \times 3^2$
$(\quad 19\quad + (\quad 5\quad)^2) \times 3^2$
$(\quad 19\quad +\quad 25\quad) \times 3^2$
$\quad\quad 44\quad\quad \times 3^2$
$\quad\quad 44\quad\quad \times 9$
$\quad\quad\quad\quad 396$

10) $((9 - 3) + (18 - 2)^2) \times 7^2$
$(\quad 6\quad + (\quad 16\quad)^2) \times 7^2$
$(\quad 6\quad +\quad 256\quad) \times 7^2$
$\quad\quad 262\quad\quad \times 7^2$
$\quad\quad 262\quad\quad \times 49$

Day 96

1) $10 + (7 \times (4 + 5)^2) + 8$
$\quad\ 10 + (7 \times\quad 9^2\quad) + 8$
$\quad\ 10 + (7 \times\quad 81\quad\ ) + 8$
$\quad\ 10 +\quad 567\qquad\ + 8$
$\qquad\qquad\qquad\qquad 585$

2) $((17 - 2) + (16 - 4)^2) \times 2^2$
$\quad (\quad 15\quad + (\quad 12\quad)^2) \times 2^2$
$\quad (\quad 15\quad +\quad 144\quad) \times 2^2$
$\qquad\qquad 159\qquad\quad \times 2^2$
$\qquad\qquad 159\qquad\quad \times 4$
$\qquad\qquad\qquad\qquad 636$

3) $((11 - 4)^2 + 5) - 8 - 2^2$
$\quad (\quad 7^2\quad + 5) - 8 - 4$
$\quad (\quad 49\quad + 5) - 8 - 4$
$\qquad\quad 54\qquad - 8 - 4$
$\qquad\qquad\qquad\qquad 42$

4) $(14 - 7)^2 + ((17 - 5) + 5^2)$
$\quad (\quad 7\quad)^2 + (\quad 12\quad + 5^2)$
$\qquad 49\quad + (\quad 12\quad + 25)$
$\qquad 49\quad +\qquad 37$
$\qquad\qquad\qquad\qquad 86$

5) $(16 - 4)^2 + ((11 - 4) + 4^2)$
$\quad (\quad 12\quad)^2 + (\quad 7\quad + 4^2)$
$\qquad 144\quad + (\quad 7\quad + 16)$
$\qquad 144\quad + \qquad 23$
$\qquad\qquad\qquad\qquad 167$

6) $((9 - 5)^2 \times 4) - 7 + 5^2$
$\quad (\quad 4^2\quad \times 4) - 7 + 25$
$\quad (\quad 16\quad \times 4) - 7 + 25$
$\qquad\quad 64\qquad - 7 + 25$
$\qquad\qquad\qquad\qquad 82$

7) $((14 + 3) + (12 - 3)^2) \times 3^2$
$\quad (\quad 17\quad + (\quad 9\quad)^2) \times 3^2$
$\quad (\quad 17\quad +\quad 81\quad) \times 3^2$
$\qquad\qquad 98\qquad\quad \times 3^2$
$\qquad\qquad 98\qquad\quad \times 9$
$\qquad\qquad\qquad\qquad 882$

8) $(4^2 + (18 - 3 + 5^2)) + 3^2$
$\quad (4^2 + (18 - 3 + 25)) + 3^2$
$\quad (4^2 + (\quad 15\quad + 25)) + 3^2$
$\quad (16 +\qquad 40\qquad) + 9$
$\qquad\quad 56\qquad\qquad + 9$
$\qquad\qquad\qquad\qquad 65$

9) $17 + (8 + (11 - 2)^2) + 8$
$\quad 17 + (8 +\quad 9^2\quad) + 8$
$\quad 17 + (8 +\quad 81\quad) + 8$
$\quad 17 +\quad 89\qquad\ + 8$
$\qquad\qquad\qquad\qquad 114$

10) $(7^2 + (12 - 4 + 5^2)) - 4^2$
$\quad (7^2 + (12 - 4 + 25)) - 4^2$
$\quad (7^2 + (\quad 8\quad + 25)) - 4^2$
$\quad (49 +\qquad 33\qquad) - 16$
$\qquad\quad 82\qquad\qquad\ 16$
$\qquad\qquad\qquad\qquad 66$

Day 97

1) $2 + (5 + (11 - 2)^2) - 8$
    $2 + (5 + \quad 9^2 \quad) - 8$
    $2 + (5 + \quad 81 \quad) - 8$
    $2 + \quad 86 \quad\quad - 8$
                    80

2) $((11 + 3) + (8 - 4)^2) \times 4^2$
    $(\quad 14 \quad + (\quad 4 \quad)^2) \times 4^2$
    $(\quad 14 \quad + \quad 16 \quad) \times 4^2$
                $30 \quad\quad \times 4^2$
                $30 \quad\quad \times 16$
                        480

3) $((6 + 2)^2 + 4) + 9 - 2^2$
    $(\quad 8^2 \quad + 4) + 9 - 4$
    $(\quad 64 \quad + 4) + 9 - 4$
            $68 \quad\quad + 9 - 4$
                        73

4) $(7^2 + (14 - 2 + 2^2)) - 5^2$
    $(7^2 + (14 - 2 + 4)) - 5^2$
    $(7^2 + (12 \quad + 4)) - 5^2$
    $(49 + \quad 16 \quad) - 25$
            $65 \quad\quad - 25$
                        40

5) $((4 + 4)^2 \times 2) + 5 - 2^2$
    $(\quad 8^2 \quad \times 2) + 5 - 4$
    $(\quad 64 \quad \times 2) + 5 - 4$
            $128 \quad\quad + 5 - 4$
                        129

6) $((17 - 6) + (12 - 3)^2) \times 6^2$
    $(\quad 11 \quad + (\quad 9 \quad)^2) \times 6^2$
    $(\quad 11 \quad + \quad 81 \quad) \times 6^2$
                $92 \quad\quad \times 6^2$
                $92 \quad\quad \times 36$
                        3312

7) $(7^2 + (20 - 2 + 3^2)) + 4^2$
    $(7^2 + (20 - 2 + 9)) + 4^2$
    $(7^2 + (18 \quad + 9)) + 4^2$
    $(49 + \quad 27 \quad) + 16$
            $76 \quad\quad + 16$
                        92

8) $(8 - 2)^2 + ((18 - 4) + 5^2)$
    $(\quad 6 \quad)^2 + (\quad 14 \quad + 5^2)$
            $36 \quad + (\quad 14 \quad + 25)$
            $36 \quad + \quad 39$
                    75

9) $18 + (8 \times (4 + 3)^2) + 7$
    $18 + (8 \times \quad 7^2 \quad) + 7$
    $18 + (8 \times \quad 49 \quad) + 7$
    $18 + \quad 392 \quad\quad + 7$
                        417

10) $(24 - 8)^2 + ((12 + 3) + 4^2)$
    $(\quad 16 \quad)^2 + (\quad 15 \quad + 4^2)$
            $256 \quad + (\quad 15 \quad + 16)$
            $256 \quad + \quad 31$
                    287

Day 98

1) $16 + (5 + (11 - 2)^2) + 8$
    $16 + (5 +\ \ \ \ \ 9^2\ \ \ \ ) + 8$
    $16 + (5 +\ \ \ \ 81\ \ \ \ ) + 8$
    $16 +\ \ \ \ \ 86\ \ \ \ \ \ \ \ \ + 8$
                       110

2) $((9 - 3) + (8 - 4)^2) \times 6^2$
    $(\ \ \ \ 6\ \ \ \ + (\ \ \ 4\ \ \ )^2) \times 6^2$
    $(\ \ \ \ 6\ \ \ +\ \ 16\ \ \ \ ) \times 6^2$
           $22\ \ \ \ \ \ \ \ \ \ \times 6^2$
           $22\ \ \ \ \ \ \ \ \ \ \times 36$
                   792

3) $4 + (9 \times (10 - 4)^2) + 6$
    $4 + (9 \times\ \ \ \ \ 6^2\ \ \ \ ) + 6$
    $4 + (9 \times\ \ \ \ 36\ \ \ \ ) + 6$
    $4 +\ \ \ \ 324\ \ \ \ \ \ \ \ + 6$
                   334

4) $(5^2 + (16 - 4 + 4^2)) - 4^2$
    $(5^2 + (16 - 4 + 16)) - 4^2$
    $(5^2 + (\ 12\ \ + 16)) - 4^2$
    $(25 +\ \ \ \ \ 28\ \ \ \ \ ) - 16$
         $53\ \ \ \ \ \ \ \ \ \ \ \ - 16$
                  37

5) $((11 - 4)^2 \times 3) + 6 - 4^2$
    $(\ \ \ 7^2\ \ \ \times 3) + 6 - 16$
    $(\ \ 49\ \ \ \ \times 3) + 6 - 16$
        $147\ \ \ \ \ + 6\ \ 16$
            137

6) $(24 -\ \ 4)^2 + ((17 + 7) \times 2^2)$
    $(\ \ \ 20\ \ )^2 + (\ \ \ 24\ \ \ \times 2^2)$
    $400\ \ \ + (\ \ \ \ 24\ \ \ \times 4\ )$
    $400\ \ +\ \ \ \ \ \ \ \ 96$
               496

7) $((13 + 7) + (16 - 4)^2) \times 2^2$
    $(\ \ \ 20\ \ \ + (\ \ 12\ \ )^2) \times 2^2$
    $(\ \ \ 20\ \ + \ 144\ \ \ ) \times 2^2$
        $164\ \ \ \ \ \ \ \ \ \times 2^2$
        $164\ \ \ \ \ \ \ \ \ \times 4$
               656

8) $((9 - 2)^2 + 7) + 5 - 2^2$
    $(\ \ \ 7^2\ \ \ + 7) + 5 - 4$
    $(\ \ 49\ \ \ \ + 7) + 5 - 4$
        $56\ \ \ \ \ + 5 - 4$
               57

9) $(15 -\ \ 3)^2 + ((17 + 7) + 5^2)$
    $(\ \ \ 12\ \ )^2 + (\ \ \ 24\ \ \ + 5^2)$
    $144\ \ \ + (\ \ \ \ 24\ \ \ + 25)$
    $144\ \ +\ \ \ \ \ \ \ \ 49$
              193

10) $(3^2 + (10 - 5 + 3^2)) + 4^2$
    $(3^2 + (10 - 5 + 9)) + 4^2$
    $(3^2 + (\ 5\ \ \ + 9)) + 4^2$
    $(9 +\ \ \ \ \ 14\ \ \ \ \ ) + 16$
        $23\ \ \ \ \ \ \ \ \ + 16$
               39

Day 99

1) $(3^2 + (15 - 5 + 4^2)) + 3^2$
   $(3^2 + (15 - 5 + 16)) + 3^2$
   $(3^2 + (\ 10\ \ + 16)) + 3^2$
   $(9\ +\ \ \ \ \ 26\ \ \ \ ) + 9$
        35   + 9
                  44

2) $9 + (2 + (9 - 5)^2) - 8$
   $9 + (2 + \ \ \ 4^2\ \ \ ) - 8$
   $9 + (2 + \ \ 16\ \ \ \ ) - 8$
   $9 + \ \ \ \ 18\ \ \ \ \ \ \ \ - 8$
                 19

3) $(18 - \ 9)^2 + ((16 - 7) \times 3^2)$
   $(\ \ 9\ \ )^2 + (\ \ \ 9\ \ \ \times 3^2)$
    81   + (9   × 9)
    81   +   81
            162

4) $((\ 4 + 3)^2 \times 6) - 10 - 4^2$
   $(\ \ 7^2\ \ \ \times 6) - 10 - 16$
   $(\ 49\ \ \ \times 6) - 10 - 16$
       294   - 10 - 16
              268

5) $14 + (2 + (4 + 2)^2) - 4$
   $14 + (2 + \ \ 6^2\ \ \ ) - 4$
   $14 + (2 + \ \ 36\ \ \ \ ) - 4$
   $14 + \ \ \ 38\ \ \ \ \ \ \ \ - 4$
               48

6) $(5^2 + (18 - 2 + 4^2)) + 3^2$
   $(5^2 + (18 - 2 + 16)) + 3^2$
   $(5^2 + (\ 16\ \ + 16)) + 3^2$
   $(25 + \ \ \ \ \ 32\ \ \ \ ) + 9$
        57   + 9
                66

7) $((14 + 5) + (10 - 2)^2) + 2^2$
   $(\ \ \ 19\ \ + (\ \ 8\ \ )^2) + 2^2$
   $(\ \ \ 19\ \ + \ \ 64\ \ \ ) + 2^2$
          83   + 2^2
          83   + 4
                87

8) $((11 - 3)^2 + 6) + 13 + 3^2$
   $(\ \ 8^2\ \ \ + 6) + 13 + 9$
   $(\ 64\ \ \ + 6) + 13 + 9$
       70   + 13 + 9
             92

9) $((15 - 5) + (18 - 2)^2) \times 4^2$
   $(\ \ 10\ \ + (\ \ 16\ \ )^2) \times 4^2$
   $(\ \ 10\ \ + \ \ 256\ \ \ ) \times 4^2$
       266   × 4^2
       266   × 16
          4256

10) $(8 - 2)^2 + ((14 + 2) \times 5^2)$
   $(\ \ 6\ \ )^2 + (\ \ 16\ \ \times 5^2)$
    36   + (16 × 25)
    36   +   400
          436

Day 100

1) $7 + (5 \times (11 - 3)^2) - 7$
    $7 + (5 \times \quad 8^2 \quad) - 7$
    $7 + (5 \times \quad 64 \quad) - 7$
    $7 + \quad 320 \quad\quad - 7$
    $\quad\quad\quad\quad\quad\quad 320$

2) $(16 - 8)^2 + ((15 - 4) + 3^2)$
    $(\quad 8 \quad)^2 + (\quad 11 \quad + 3^2)$
    $\quad 64 \quad + (\quad 11 \quad + 9)$
    $\quad 64 \quad + \quad\quad 20$
    $\quad\quad\quad\quad\quad 84$

3) $(20 - 5)^2 + ((9 - 3) + 4^2)$
    $(\quad 15 \quad)^2 + (\quad 6 \quad + 4^2)$
    $\quad 225 \quad + (\quad 6 \quad + 16)$
    $\quad 225 \quad + \quad\quad 22$
    $\quad\quad\quad\quad\quad 247$

4) $((16 + 4) + (10 - 5)^2) \times 6^2$
    $(\quad 20 \quad + (\quad 5 \quad)^2) \times 6^2$
    $(\quad 20 \quad + \quad 25 \quad) \times 6^2$
    $\quad\quad 45 \quad\quad\quad \times 6^2$
    $\quad\quad 45 \quad\quad\quad \times 36$
    $\quad\quad\quad\quad\quad 1620$

5) $7 + (6 + (5 + 3)^2) - 5$
    $7 + (6 + \quad 8^2 \quad) - 5$
    $7 + (6 + \quad 64 \quad) - 5$
    $7 + \quad 70 \quad\quad\quad 5$
    $\quad\quad\quad\quad 72$

6) $((4 + 3)^2 \times 2) - 8 + 5^2$
    $(\quad 7^2 \quad \times 2) - 8 + 25$
    $(\quad 49 \quad \times 2) - 8 + 25$
    $\quad\quad 98 \quad\quad - 8 + 25$
    $\quad\quad\quad\quad\quad 115$

7) $(3^2 + (8 - 4 + 4^2)) - 2^2$
    $(3^2 + (8 - 4 + 16)) - 2^2$
    $(3^2 + (4 + 16)) - 2^2$
    $(9 + \quad 20 \quad) - 4$
    $\quad\quad 29 \quad\quad - 4$
    $\quad\quad\quad\quad 25$

8) $((17 + 7) + (12 - 3)^2) \times 5^2$
    $(\quad 24 \quad + (\quad 9 \quad)^2) \times 5^2$
    $(\quad 24 \quad + \quad 81 \quad) \times 5^2$
    $\quad\quad\quad 105 \quad\quad \times 5^2$
    $\quad\quad\quad 105 \quad\quad \times 25$
    $\quad\quad\quad\quad\quad 2625$

9) $(3^2 + (24 - 2 + 4^2)) + 3^2$
    $(3^2 + (24 - 2 + 16)) + 3^2$
    $(3^2 + (22 + 16)) + 3^2$
    $(9 + \quad 38 \quad) + 9$
    $\quad\quad 47 \quad\quad\quad + 9$
    $\quad\quad\quad\quad 56$

10) $((5 + 3)^2 + 7) - 10 + 6^2$
    $(\quad 8^2 \quad + 7) - 10 + 36$
    $(\quad 64 \quad + 7) - 10 + 36$
    $\quad\quad 71 \quad\quad - 10 + 36$
    $\quad\quad\quad\quad 97$

Made in United States
Orlando, FL
13 May 2024

46814618R00115